THE AMERICAN CIVIL WAR

WARFARE THROUGH THE CENTURIES

Paul Brewer

ROSEN PUBLISHING

Published in 2025 by The Rosen Publishing Group, Inc.
2544 Clinton Street, Buffalo, NY 14224

Editor: Ashley Brown
Designer: John Woolford

Cataloging-in-Publication Data

Names: Brewer, Paul.
Title: The American civil war / Paul Brewer.
Description: New York: Rosen Publishing, 2025. | Series: Warfare through the centuries | Includes glossary, index, and bibliographic information
Identifiers: ISBN 9781499478709 (pbk) | ISBN 9781499478716 (library bound) | ISBN 9781499478723 (ebook)
Subjects: LCSH: Military history, Modern—juvenile literature | Military art and science—juvenile literature | United States—History—Civil War, 1861-1865—juvenile literature
Classification: LCC E468 .B74 2025 | DDC 973.7--dc24

PICTURE SOURCES
Front Cover: Library of Congress.
Interior: Alamy: Granger Historical Picture Archive 76; Library of Congress: 1, 5, 9, 10, 12, 24, 29, 30, 34, 36, 38, 40, 41, 43, 50, 52, 55, 56, 58, 59, 64, 67, 68, 69, 71, 73, 75; Look and Learn: 47, 48; NARA: 6, 14, 33; National Portrait Gallery: 20; Open Access: Missouri History Museum 32; Public Domain: 26, Matthew Benjamin Brady 17, Encyclopedia Virginia 18, Famous Leaders and Battle Scenes of the Civil War, Frank Leslie 13, Heritage Auctions 77, New York Public Library Digital Collection 16, The Photographic History of the Civil War 63, Yale University Art Gallery 21; Shutterstock: Everett Collection 60; United States Government: National Park Service/NPS 54.

All other photography and artwork Brown Bear Books.

Some of the images in this book illustrate individuals who are models. The depictions do not imply actual situations or events.

Manufactured in the United States of America

CPSIA Compliance Information: Batch #CW25RYA. For further information, contact Rosen Publishing, New York, New York, at 1-800-237-9932.

CONTENTS

Introduction

The American Civil War was fought between 1861 and 1865 between Northern states who wanted enslaved people to be free and Southern states supporting slavery. It remains a key event in the history of the United States, for the outcome of the Civil War laid the foundations for the political, military, and economic might of the modern nation. Victory for President Abraham Lincoln and his armies, which in the war fought under the banner of the United States, made sure this country would remain a single, undivided nation without slavery.

In military terms the Civil War was also a key event. Changes in the ways that later wars were fought, in terms of technology, and in the makeup of armies could be seen elsewhere, particularly in Europe, but the Civil War brought them into sharp focus.

Above all the Civil War was the first industrial war. It was one in which modern industrial processes, such as mass production, harnessed to relatively new technologies, including the railroad and telegraphy, decided the outcome as much as the soldiers' and generals' skills. The Civil War was the first modern "total war," a conflict in which both sides used all of their principal resources, both human and economic, to win a complete victory. By modern standards the Confederacy (pro-slavery states) was at a disadvantage. It had a smaller population, a much less developed industrial base, and fewer miles of railroad. It also had few warships. However, in 1861 these disadvantages seemed outweighed by the South's advantage in the quality of its soldiers and the skills of its generals. Many believed that if the South could inflict a major defeat on the North or capture Washington, D.C., quickly, then the war might be won by the South. However, the Union, with its vast reserves of manpower and huge industrial output, could replace its losses. The Confederacy could not. The Union armies also became more efficient and began to be led by top generals. The Confederacy needed to win quickly. When it failed to do so, the war was inevitably lost.

The Civil War highlighted the great power of many new weapons. Muskets had a longer range and greater accuracy than previously. The repeating rifle allowed a soldier to fire several shots a minute rather than the usual two or three. Artillery with greater firepower and range was being introduced. So great was the increase in firepower that charges by both cavalrymen and infantry units virtually disappeared. Casualties in the face of such firepower would have been too great.

The soldiers who carried these new weapons had to suffer the impact of their use. The Civil War remains the most deadly war in the history of the United States. Northern military casualties totaled nearly 260,000 dead, while the Confederacy suffered close to 250,000 dead. This slaughter reflected the use of new weapons, but over 300,000 of the total fatalities died from other causes, chiefly disease, infection, and poor medical treatment

The Civil War Begins

The first shots of the American Civil War were fired at Fort Sumter in April 1861. The newly elected president, Abraham Lincoln, knew that many people in the North were unwilling to take up arms to fight their fellow Americans. He also knew that many Americans were not unduly bothered by slavery. Although Lincoln was opposed to an extension of slavery in the United States, he justified the war on different grounds—the preservation of the Union. His oath of office demanded that he bring the Southern states back into the Union.

All of the United States allowed slavery—the right for some human beings to own others—when the United States declared its independence from Britain in 1776. However, in 1808, buying slaves from outside the United States was prohibited in all states by federal law. By 1815, all the states north of Maryland and the Ohio River had passed laws to end slavery either immediately or gradually. These

Confederate shells rain down on the walls of U.S.-held Fort Sumter in Charleston Harbor, South Carolina, April 1861.

Harriet Beecher Stowe's book *Uncle Tom's Cabin*, published in 1862, revealed the horrors of slavery and shocked many of its readers.

changes led to a divided economy. The wealthy in the South had large farms, called plantations, which depended heavily on enslaved labor.

In the North workers on farms or in factories or other jobs were free to quit when they chose.

For and Against Slavery

A number of people in the North, especially in New England, believed that slavery was wrong. Chief among these were many devout Christians. Other men and women also saw slavery as evil. Harriet Beecher Stowe's novel *Uncle Tom's Cabin*, which highlighted the evils of slavery, was widely read in the North. Politicians from the North began to argue in favor of ending slavery, an action known as abolition. However, there were enough proslavery politicians to vote down any threat to slavery. Beginning with the so-called Missouri Compromise of 1820, almost every time a state outlawing slavery entered the Union, a proslavery one was allowed to join.

During the 1850s the growth of the nation gradually favored the free states over the slave ones. In those territories edging toward statehood, there were violent clashes between pro- and antislavery groups. During the settlement of Kansas, for example, the violence between the factions was so bad that the territory was called "Bleeding Kansas." Southerners fought to force slavery on Kansas, but in 1858 Kansas voted against slavery.

In 1859, John Brown, one of the abolitionist leaders in Kansas, attempted to start a slave revolt in Virginia. He led a small group of abolitionists that seized the U.S. arsenal at Harpers Ferry, Virginia. However, the authorities sent a detachment of troops to deal with the abolitionist and his followers. Brown was captured and he was hanged for treason. This incident convinced the South's political leaders that they had to secure the future of slavery at the presidential election in 1860.

Members of the Democratic Party were united in their belief that enslavers should be allowed to take enslaved people into the western territories and believed that Congress did not have the right to ban slavery in the territories.

They also supported the 1850 Fugitive Slave Act, which ordered that enslaved people who ran away but were captured in states without slavery should be returned.

However, the Democrats were split on other issues. Southern Democrats wanted a slave code to explicitly protect slavery in the territories. Northern Democrats believed that slavery should be a matter left up to the territorial legislatures but also supported any decision the U.S. Supreme Court might make on the status of slavery in the territories or the power of the territorial legislatures on the subject. The Northern and Southern Democrats were deeply divided. Both put forward presidential candidates.

A Nation Divided

In the election of 1860, there were four candidates for president. The Northern Democrats chose Stephen Douglas of Illinois. The Southern Democrats nominated Vice President John Breckinridge of Kentucky. The Republicans, who opposed slavery in any territory, named Abraham Lincoln of Illinois.

Constitutional Unionists, who took no position on the slavery issue, nominated John Bell from Tennessee. The Southern Democrats and the Constitutional Unionists gambled that no single candidate would receive a majority of the electoral college votes. The Southern Democrats believed that the House of Representatives, voting by states, would then choose the new president.

However, on November 6, 1860, Lincoln won a clear majority of the electoral votes. These votes were all from the North only. In response, on December 20 a proslavery convention meeting in South Carolina voted to leave the Union, or secede. Lincoln was inaugurated as president, on March 4, 1861, by which time South Carolina had been joined by Georgia, Florida, Alabama, Mississippi, Louisiana,

Abraham Lincoln was opposed to the spread of slavery. When he became president in 1861, proslavery politicians in the South decided to leave the Union.

and Texas. These seven proslavery states formed the Confederate States of America and elected Jefferson Davis from Mississippi as their president. Newly elected President Lincoln faced a crisis that could have led to the end of the United States.

Flashpoint at Fort Sumter

Most U.S. forts and naval dockyards in the states that had seceded surrendered to the Confederates. Four forts held out, including Fort Sumter in Charleston Harbor, South Carolina. Lincoln regarded the forts as federal property. While hoping to avoid war, he felt any attempt by a state government to grab federal property was an act of insurrection. If such an event took place, Lincoln would use the army to invade the seceded states and restore federal authority.

An unarmed U.S. merchant ship, *Star of the World*, under direct orders from outgoing President Buchanan had attempted to reinforce Fort Sumter with troops and supplies. On January 9, 1861, it was driven off by gunfire from the South Carolina shore. But there was no actual attack against the fort itself until April. Sumter became an issue when, on the 11th, the Confederate forces in Charleston demanded the surrender of Sumter's U.S. garrison. The commander of the U.S. garrison, Major Robert Anderson, born in the South, refused. On the 12th, a bombardment of the fort began that lasted for 34 hours. Anderson had no hope of getting help, and under the intense shelling felt he had no option but to surrender the fort.

When Lincoln heard of the surrender of Fort Sumter, on April

CONFEDERATE DIPLOMACY

Confederate political leaders knew very well that the United States had more factories, more money, and a larger population. These three advantages would eventually lead to the defeat of the seceding states. The Confederates had studied history, however, and realized that the North American colonies had won their revolution against Britain in the late 18th century with the help of European countries, especially France.

Southern leader Jefferson Davis tried to get the most powerful countries in Europe to recognize his government as an independent state. This would make it much easier for the Confederate government to borrow money, and offered the possibility of an alliance with one of the European powers.

Davis's strategy began with the South halting the export of cotton to Europe. Davis hoped the Europeans would recognize the Confederacy in exchange for the supply of cotton being resumed. This failed because the European countries turned elsewhere, chiefly India and Egypt, for their cotton. The South's supply of cotton to Europe was resumed, but the cotton trade then suffered due to the Union naval blockade of Southern ports.

THE WAR BETWEEN THE NORTH AND SOUTH

This map shows the major battles of the Civil War, as well as the Union naval blockade that helped to crush the South. Both the Union and Confederacy wanted a short war. If the war did not end quickly, the South had little chance of winning or gaining a favorable peace settlement.

14, he called for 75,000 militiamen to serve for three months to suppress the rebellion. Later, when it became clear that the war would not be over quickly, he would ask for three-year enlistments.

Lincoln's chief aim was to preserve the Union and, if this meant going to war, he would do so. In response to Lincoln's decision the states of Virginia, North Carolina, Tennessee, and Arkansas joined the Confederacy, although some people from Virginia and Tennessee did fight for the North. Part of Virginia opted to leave the Confederacy and was allowed to enter the Union as a new state, West Virginia, in 1863. Neither the South nor the North, however, was aware of just how long the war that followed would last.

Unequal Resources

The distribution of major resources, both human and economic, suggested on paper at least that the North would have little difficulty in dealing with the Confederacy. Those states remaining loyal to the United States contained most of the nation's industry, railroads, and gold reserves, and had a population of 22 million. The Confederates had only five million whites. Over three million African Americans living in the South were very unlikely to fight to remain slaves. Many African Americans, some 200,000 by the end of the war, fought for the North and most had fled proslavery states. The bulk of the U.S. Navy and much of the regular army remained loyal to the United States.

However, the South did have some advantages. About one-third of the regular U.S. Army's officers remained loyal to their birthplaces and resigned to fight for the Confederacy, although most of the Southern-born U.S. Army's ordinary soldiers remained loyal to the United States.

The South could move armies on "interior lines." This meant that, like the spokes of a wheel, the Southern armies could be concentrated in the hub (center), around Richmond. It would be shorter and quicker to move them along the spokes from the center. Northern troops would most likely be in positions along the rim of the "wheel" and have much farther to travel around it. Although the South's troops were outnumbered

Jefferson Davis was elected the provisional president of the Confederate States of America on February 9, 1861.

THE ANACONDA PLAN

The General-in-Chief of the U.S. Army, Winfield Scott, was a former presidential candidate, a hero of the Mexican-American War, and a Virginian. He revealed in a letter to a subordinate dated May 3, 1861, a plan for defeating the Confederate states. Scott wanted to attack along the Mississippi River from inland and from the sea. A large army would advance from southern Illinois, while part of the navy brought troops to capture New Orleans.

The rest of the Union navy would blockade, or prevent ships from entering or leaving, Confederate ports. The federal blockade and control of the Mississippi would disrupt the Southern economy and split the seceding states in two. The newspapers named Scott's strategy the "Anaconda Plan," after a big snake that slowly crushes its prey in its coils.

During the first months of the Civil War, U.S. forces carried out some key parts of the plan. Troops captured islands at Hatteras Inlet off North Carolina and established a base to blockade Southern ports in August. Port Royal, South Carolina, from where Union ships could menace Charleston and Savannah, was taken in November. Similar successes followed in 1862, particularly the capture of New Orleans, Louisiana, by Admiral David Farragut on April 24–25.

in total by the Union armies, they could rely on movement by railroad down these interior lines to gain a local advantage in numbers. This was a strategy that would allow the Southern armies to react quickly to any Northern advance into the Confederacy and often have enough men in position to defeat a major Union attack.

Hopes of Quick Victory

Facing the greater resources of the North, the new president of the Confederacy, Jefferson Davis, adopted a defensive strategy. He hoped that quick Confederate military successes against the Union would lead to the recognition of the Confederacy by powerful foreign countries, especially Britain and France. He also hoped that many of those in the North would agree on a peace settlement favorable to the South if their armies were defeated or Washington, D.C., was menaced or even captured by Southern forces.

With hindsight the outcome of the Civil War actually hinged on whether the Confederates' determination to keep their independence would be maintained long enough to offset the superior industrial power and human resources of the North. However, early in 1861, the politicians of the North and South believed that a war, if it came, would involve very few battles and be over shortly. Both sets of leaders were to be proved wrong.

The First Battles

With the fall of Fort Sumter, all-out war had become very likely. Both Union and Confederacy now began a race to take over those states that had not yet decided which side to join. Then, as both North and South prepared for military action, both also faced a problem in that there were few professional soldiers available. Raw recruits or state militias would form the manpower for the armies that were being built up. Many of these men were enthusiastic but knew little of war. The early battles proved that enthusiasm was not enough.

Lincoln's request for 75,000 volunteers to serve for three months in April 1861 also allowed the Confederates 20 days to return to the Union. This period was due to expire on May 5. On May 3, the Confederates, meeting at Montgomery, Alabama, adopted an act "recognizing the existence of war between the United States and the Confederate States." Southern president Jefferson Davis signed the act on May 6. This made war inevitable, but there were some U.S. states that had not yet declared their allegiance.

General Sterling Price fought the first battle of the Civil War when he led Missouri militia against Union forces.

Attempts to Prevent Secession

In three states—Maryland, Kentucky, and Missouri—the balance between U.S. and Confederate forces was almost equal. Lincoln refused to allow Confederate supporters in Maryland to attempt to bring about secession. He suspended habeas corpus, the right of prisoners to have their imprisonment reviewed by a judge. This suspension is allowed by the Constitution in "Cases of Rebellion or Invasion."

THE FIRST VOLUNTEERS

Until 1861 the United States relied on voluntary units of ordinary citizens organized by their states to provide much of its military force. Militia officers were elected and their part-timers assembled on weekends or holidays.

At the start of the Civil War the Confederacy and the United States called for volunteers. In each case the peacetime militia units provided the basis.

The 75,000 volunteers asked for by Lincoln in April 1861 were largely provided by these people. Many were immigrants to the United States from Ireland and Germany. While they were enthusiastic, they were not trained soldiers.

Both the North and South soon realized that they would need more soldiers. The South moved first. In April 1862, the government passed a law proclaiming that all able-bodied white males between 18–35 were liable for active military service. The North followed on July 17.

Laws making military service compulsory were not always popular. There were serious riots against them, for example, in both Baltimore and New York, but both sides needed trained, long-serving soldiers to fight the war.

Union troops in the uniforms worn by some volunteer units in the early stages of the war.

In Kentucky and Missouri, however, Lincoln did not act so forcefully. He quietly organized a pro-Union movement in Kentucky, where the governor was trying to keep his state neutral. In Missouri, the governor, Claiborne Jackson, a Confederate sympathizer, had been in secret communication with Jefferson Davis over ways to bring the state into the Confederacy.

During the spring of 1861 a strange situation developed in Missouri. Governor Jackson called up the militia to defend his state against the U.S. government of which it was still a part. Meanwhile, President Lincoln appointed a group of men to wage war against the government of Missouri, a state that his oath required him to defend. Street fighting broke out in St. Louis on May 10. The state legislature—which had been anti-rebellion—authorized Jackson to act against Lincoln's men.

After some unsuccessful negotiations U.S. Brigadier General Nathaniel Lyon advanced from St. Louis to the state capital, Jefferson City, and drove the governor out of the city on June 14. The first major battle of the Civil War was fought at nearby Boonville two days later. Lyon's troops defeated a smaller force of pro-Confederate Missouri militia. Claiborne Jackson and his militia commander, General Sterling Price, fled to the southwest of the state. Missouri had been kept in the Union.

Meanwhile, the Confederates had voted to move their capital from Montgomery, Alabama, to Richmond, Virginia. The Confederate government and the Lincoln administration in Washington, D.C., now faced one another across little more than 100 miles (160 km) of land in the state of Virginia.

First Major Battle

U.S. General Irvin McDowell now put before Lincoln a plan to attack the Confederates around Manassas Junction in Virginia. The Confederates at the little town of Manassas were ready to launch an attack on Washington. If the federal forces defeated the Southern troops at Manassas, the vital railroad junction linking Richmond with the Shenandoah Valley, an important grain-producing area, would be denied to the South.

McDowell's army marched on July 16. McDowell had 38,000 troops under his command, but only 2,000 were regulars. Two days later McDowell found Confederate troops, again mostly militia, commanded by General P. G. T.

General Pierre Beauregard was from Louisiana and oversaw the bombardment of Fort Sumter in April 1861. At the First Battle of Bull Run in July 1861 he was second in command to General Joseph E. Johnston.

THE FIRST BATTLE OF BULL RUN

Beauregard defending the Bull Run River. McDowell decided to outflank Beauregard's position by sending most of his forces sweeping around the Confederates. McDowell believed Beauregard commanded just 20,000 men. He did not know that 12,000 troops commanded by General Joseph E. Johnston were rushing to Manassas.

The battle, known as First Bull Run (or First Manassas), took place on July 21, 1861. People from Washington came to watch the battle. The federal attack caught the Confederates by surprise.

The bulk of their army was still several hours' march south of where McDowell's attacked.

Confederate Reinforcements Arrive

However, the inexperience of the federal troops prevented them from striking a decisive blow against the Confederates. This gave time for reinforcements to rush from other parts of the Confederate line, and for others to arrive from the Shenandoah Valley. A brigade of Virginians commanded by General Thomas Jackson provided a rallying point at the top of Henry House Hill, the weakest part of the South's line. One Southern officer described Jackson's men as standing like a "stone wall" in the face of the Union attacks. "Stonewall" very soon became Jackson's nickname.

McDowell gathered his troops for one more attack, but Confederate reinforcements outflanked the Union line, and the whole federal army began to retreat. When a wagon overturned at Cub Run Bridge, blocking the federal troops' line of retreat, the undisciplined soldiers threw down their weapons and fled in terror.

The Fight for Missouri

Meanwhile, in Missouri, General Nathaniel Lyon had advanced southwestward from Jefferson City to the town of Springfield with an army of about 7,000 men. At the beginning of August, he decided to attack a larger Confederate army at Wilson's Creek, also in Missouri. The Confederates were commanded by General Sterling Price and General Ben McCulloch. Their

A European cartoon showing General Irvin McDowell's forces streaming away in disorder from the battlefield at the First Battle of Bull Run.

McCLELLAN AND THE ARMY OF THE POTOMAC

General George B. McClellan was affectionately known by the soldiers he commanded as "Little Mac." He was born in Philadelphia and had graduated first in the West Point class of 1846. He was a hero of the Mexican-American War, and when that ended in 1848, he held many important assignments in the army. He earned a reputation for intelligence and efficiency.

McClellan was an obvious candidate to command a Union army. He won battles at the beginning of the war, and his friendship with General Winfield Scott, the overall commander of all the Union forces, helped him to get command of the Army of the Potomac in July 1861.

When McClellan arrived in Washington to take command of the Army of the Potomac, he took over a defeated rabble. By training his men, and by speaking to them at massed parades, he made them feel proud to be soldiers again. The Army of the Potomac would always have a special place in its heart for "Little Mac." McClellan was, however, far too cautious and later faced one of the greatest military minds of the day, the South's General Robert E. Lee. McClellan was relieved of his command in November 1862 by President Lincoln.

General George McClellan was a brilliant organizer, but his caution led President Lincoln to replace him.

armies were very badly equipped, but ready for a fight. The battle, fought on August 10, ended in a narrow Confederate victory, but the Southerners were far too exhausted to capitalize on their victory at Wilson's Creek and Missouri remained in federal hands.

McClellan Takes Charge

The only battlefield success for the federal side in the first summer of the war came in what was to become West Virginia. General George B. McClellan won a victory in the Battle of Rich Mountain on July 11. Partly as a result, he was appointed in McDowell's place on July 22. McClellan realized that he would have to train his new command, the Army of the Potomac, to fight as well as any regular troops. A federal defeat, at Ball's Bluff, near Leesburg in Virginia, on October 21, reinforced this view. The future of the war effort lay with the soldiers who had enlisted for three years. It was dawning on commanders that the war would last for a long time.

Richmond Attacked

The Confederate victory at the First Battle of Bull Run in July 1861 did not lead to any significant Southern advantage. The Confederate army was too weak to risk a march on Washington. On the Union side, General George McClellan was unwilling to attack the South with his troops until they had had the training to improve their battlefield skills. Both sides remained in their camps until March 1862. At this point, however, McClellan was ready to launch an offensive against the Southern capital, Richmond.

In the spring of 1862 things began to happen quickly. McClellan had planned to maneuver the Confederate army, now commanded by General Joseph E. Johnston, away from Manassas Junction. However, Johnston was already abandoning his defenses there. Jefferson Davis wanted the main Confederate army in Virginia nearer the capital at Richmond just in case the Union troops attempted to invade the South by sea.

McClellan reached Johnston's abandoned positions in Virginia and drew up a new campaign plan. He would ship a very large army down the Chesapeake Bay to Fort Monroe, near Norfolk, Virginia. This stronghold was still in Union hands and would provide an excellent base for operations. From Fort Monroe the Union forces could attack Richmond from the southeast. It was exactly the plan Davis had feared. In the meantime McClellan placed a force of about 10,000 soldiers at Winchester,

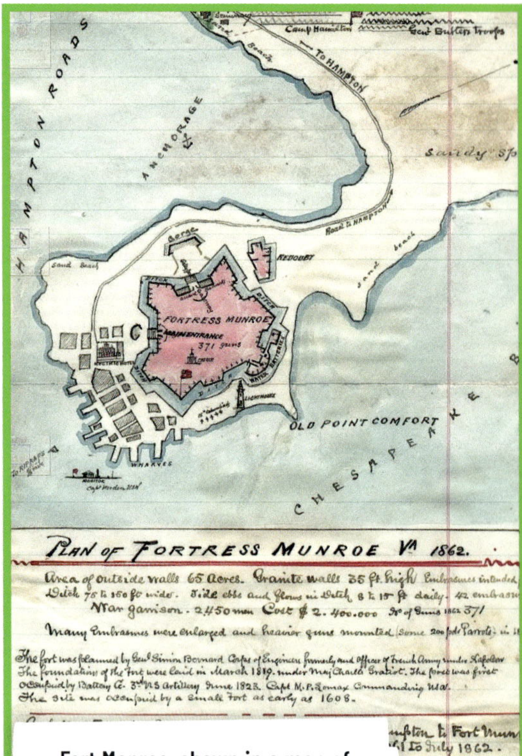

Fort Monroe, shown in a map of 1862. General McClellan intended to use it to disembark a large army that would sweep east toward Richmond.

THOMAS J. "STONEWALL" JACKSON

Thomas Jackson was born in Clarksburg, Virginia, in 1824 and graduated from West Point in 1846. He served with distinction in the Mexican-American War before he became an instructor in artillery tactics and natural philosophy at the Virginia Military Institute in 1852. When the Civil War began, he was commissioned as a colonel of volunteers and was then promoted to the rank of brigadier general in June 1861.

Jackson was a great general but a hard taskmaster. Soldiers who served under him were pushed to the limit of their abilities, but his troops often found that little extra reserve of moral strength that made the difference between victory and defeat.

However, the extent to which Jackson drove himself and his troops probably cost Robert E. Lee a greater victory during the Seven Days Campaign (see pages 22–23) in 1862. Both Jackson and his troops were exhausted by their campaign in the Shenandoah Valley, and they did not perform to the best of their abilities.

Jackson was accidentally shot by one of his own soldiers at the Battle of Chancellorsville in May 1863. The death of this great battlefield commander was a major blow to the Confederacy.

Virginia, to protect a railroad line running west from Washington to the Ohio River. It was commanded by Brigadier General James Shields. The Confederates there numbered about 5,000 troops, commanded by Stonewall Jackson, guarding the Shenandoah Valley.

War in Virginia

Jackson made one attempt to attack Shields's force, at Kernstown, Virginia, on March 23. However, Jackson did not have enough troops to break through the strong Union defenses and was forced to retreat. Jackson's attack at Kernstown, despite being a failure, had a major impact on the campaign that was to follow. McClellan's Union troops were already marching to the coast and embarking on ships to be ferried south to Fort Monroe. But Lincoln had only given permission for the plan to go ahead if Washington was securely defended. He ordered McClellan to leave behind 30,000 of the soldiers that McClellan had expected to take with him to Fort Monroe. Lincoln's concern over Jackson's supposed threat to Washington greatly weakened McClellan's main army.

This division of the Union forces might not have been important, except that McClellan believed that he faced a much larger Confederate army than was actually the case. While there were about 15,000 Confederate troops between the Union forces and Richmond, McClellan guessed at roughly double that number.

McClellan was afraid of being attacked and he made the 20-mile (32 km) march between Fort

Monroe and Yorktown very slowly. The Confederate garrison at Yorktown remained in place to buy time for the main Confederate army in Virginia to place itself between McClellan and Richmond.

McClellan could not allow Yorktown to remain in Confederate hands so he took his time constructing siege works around the port. Eventually, on May 3–4, the Confederate defenders of Yorktown under General John Magruder headed for Richmond. McClellan had lost valuable time. Jefferson Davis and General Johnston were still worried. They believed that Richmond would have

General Joseph E. Johnston. Commanding Confederate troops facing the forces of McClellan, he was wounded in May 1862 and replaced by Robert E. Lee.

A painting by Winslow Homer depicting troops in their encampment outside Yorktown. The slowness of Union movements allowed the Confederacy to defeat McClellan's 1862 offensive.

to be abandoned if the Union armies combined their numbers and advanced together.

Jackson's Campaign

The Union forces were large. There were troops in West Virginia commanded by General John C. Frémont; General Nathaniel Banks had 30,000 Union soldiers in the Shenandoah Valley; while about 75,000 Union troops around Washington and near Fredericksburg were taking orders from U.S. Secretary of War Edwin M. Stanton and President Lincoln. Meanwhile, McClellan had about 100,000 soldiers of the Army of the Potomac in place around Yorktown and Fort Monroe.

Johnston, Davis, and Davis's military adviser, General Robert E. Lee, ordered Jackson to attack Banks, and, if he felt he had time, Frémont as well. The fighting that followed, known as Jackson's Valley Campaign (May 1–June 9), was one of the most outstanding efforts of the whole war.

On May 8, Jackson struck at part of Frémont's army in the south of the Shenandoah Valley. Frémont was caught off guard, and afterward proceeded cautiously when what was needed most was boldness. Jackson marched north, heading for Winchester, Virginia, and on May 23 surprised Union troops at Front Royal. Banks had not expected Jackson to come that way. He decided to retreat to Winchester. The race between the two was won by Banks, but he was unable to beat Jackson on May 25.

JACKSON'S VALLEY CAMPAIGN

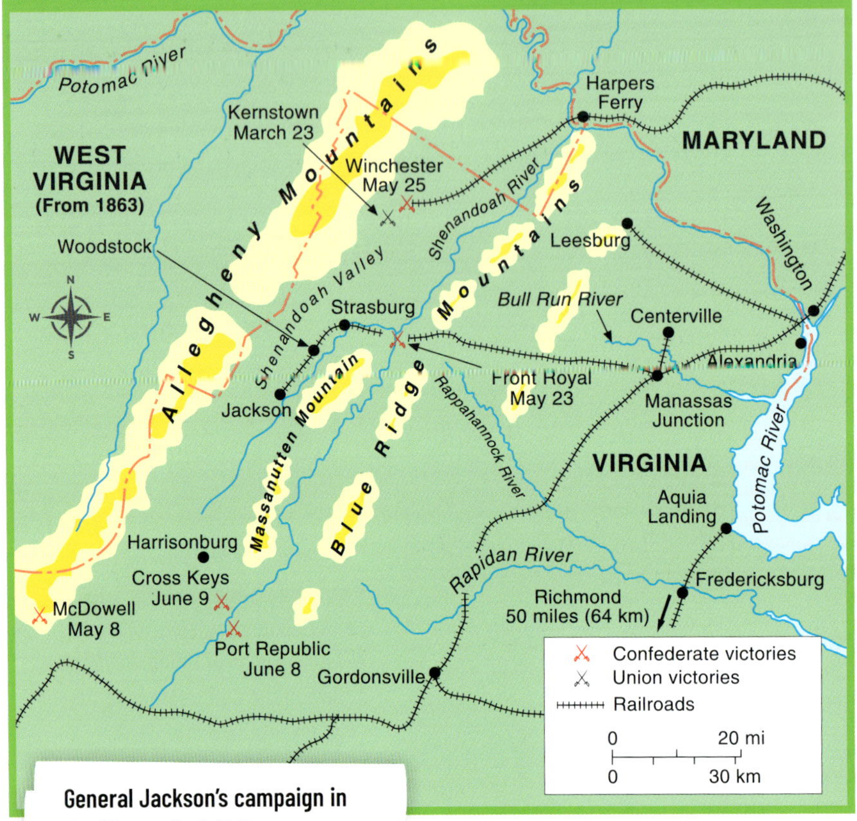

General Jackson's campaign in the Shenandoah Valley was fought in May and June 1862. It was conducted with great skill against superior Union forces and prevented Northern generals from concentrating their superior troop numbers against Richmond, the Southern capital.

Jackson's Confederates were now able to capture Winchester. This success greatly worried the politicians in Washington.

Lincoln and Stanton, fearing that Jackson was about to attack Washington, ordered General Irvin McDowell to send troops under Shields to the Shenandoah Valley. They also ordered Frémont to advance northeastward back toward Washington. Jackson, they hoped, would be caught between these two forces.

Success for Jackson

Jackson, however, used his position between the two Union forces to his advantage. First, his troops defeated Shields at Port Republic on June 8, then he turned and repulsed Frémont's attack at Cross Keys on the following day. Having fought a brilliant campaign in the Shenandoah Valley, Jackson now took the bulk of his army back toward Richmond.

The Seven Days Campaign ended in a Southern victory that stopped the Union forces from capturing Richmond.

THE SEVEN DAYS CAMPAIGN

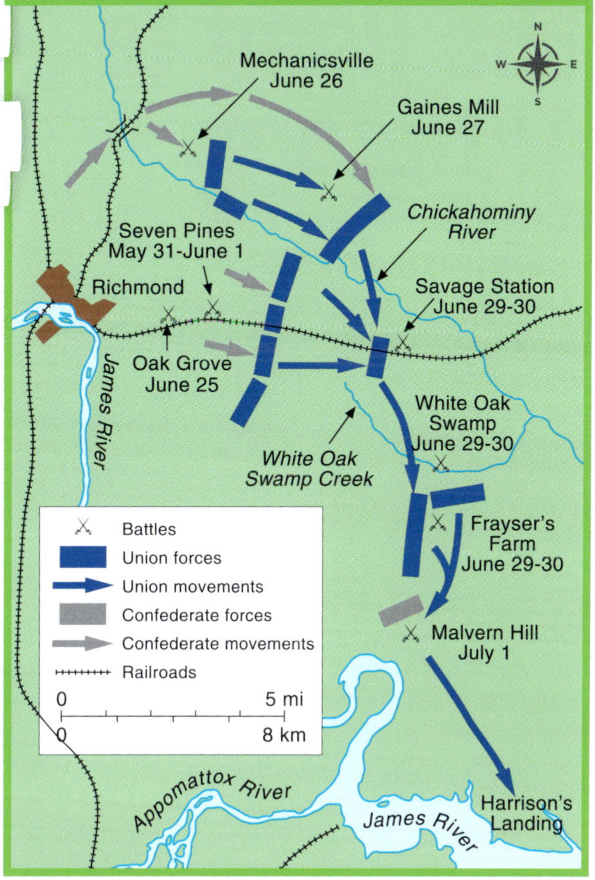

The Seven Days Campaign

Johnston's army had attacked McClellan's forces at the Battle of Seven Pines (also known as the Battle of Fair Oaks) outside Richmond on May 31. The battle was a draw, and Johnston was wounded. Lee then took charge of the main Southern force, the Army of Northern Virginia. Seven Pines caused McClellan to stop. He mistakenly believed he was outnumbered. Lee waited three weeks for Jackson to return from the Shenandoah Valley, then attacked McClellan.

In a series of bitter battles fought between June 25 and July 1, known as the Seven Days Campaign, Lee succeeded in forcing the Union army to retreat. Many of the battles, including Mechanicsville (June 26) and Gaines Mill (the 27th), did not result in clear-cut Confederate victories, but were strategic successes because the Union troops were forced to retreat southward toward the James River.

Richmond Saved

The last battle of the campaign, fought at Malvern Hill, to the north of the James River, on July 1, was a Union victory, however. Lee launched his troops against Union defenses on the hill's slopes and suffered over 5,000 casualties in just two hours. This Confederate defeat allowed the Union forces to retreat to Harrison's Landing, where they were protected by Union warships. Richmond was now safe. In August McClellan sailed for Washington, his grand plan having failed.

The Road to Antietam

The Confederate leadership had defended Richmond successfully in June 1862. It began to plan a major invasion of the North. The leadership hoped that a victory would lead to the fall of Washington and persuade the Union to recognize the Confederacy as an independent state. This campaign was to be led by General Robert E. Lee, the new commander of the Army of Northern Virginia. Lee's plan of campaign relied heavily on the troops led by General Stonewall Jackson, the hero of the First Battle of Bull Run.

If the South was encouraged by the defense of Richmond, the Union command was in poor shape. Union commander George McClellan had made many promises to President Lincoln, but his attempt to capture Richmond in the first half of 1862 had been a disaster. McClellan blamed everyone but himself, yet it was his slowness of maneuver against an enemy inferior in numbers that cost the Union its best chance to capture the South's capital. Lincoln decided that he needed some new army commanders to take control of the campaign in Virginia.

Lincoln believed that the divided Union leadership in the Shenandoah Valley and the lack of an overall commander of Union forces in the eastern theater of operations contributed to McClellan's failure. He brought two commanders who had won battles in Tennessee and along the Mississippi River to Washington with the intention of promoting both. General Henry Halleck was given overall command of federal

General Robert E. Lee, one of the greatest commanders of the Civil War.

GENERAL ROBERT E. LEE

Robert E. Lee was possibly the most admired officer in the U.S. Army at the beginning of 1861. He had graduated from West Point second in the class of 1829 and served as an engineer officer in the Mexican-American War.

Later he had been the superintendent of West Point and commander of a cavalry regiment and he was offered command of the Union armies in April 1861. But he left all this behind because his home state of Virginia had left the Union to join the Confederacy. It took a year, though, before he was given a major field command. However, he then proved himself one of the best commanders of the war. He had a brilliant grasp of strategy, was methodical in laying plans, and always reacted to difficult situations with great calm and thought.

Lee's troops loved him and refused to allow him to risk his life. At Gettysburg in 1863, after the defeat of Pickett's Charge, which made sure that the battle would end in a Union victory, he rode among the survivors saying, "It is all my fault." As a general, Lee took daring gambles that often succeeded. After the Civil War he became president of Washington College in Lexington, Virginia.

forces in Virginia, while General John Pope was placed in charge of the Union troops in the Shenandoah Valley.

An Attacking Commander

Pope was a commander who wanted to attack, something that Lincoln knew McClellan did not like to do. But when Pope arrived, he issued a proclamation to his troops that suggested they were not as good as the soldiers he had led in Tennessee. The Union troops believed he had no confidence in them. Their morale, or their belief that they had a chance to win a battle, was therefore damaged. Pope thought their morale would improve if he got them to advance. So he began moving toward a vital railroad junction at Gordonsville, Virginia. Halleck also ordered McClellan to return with his army to the Washington area.

General Robert E. Lee learned what was happening. He left Richmond and advanced on Pope's army. Lee guessed Halleck's plan. He knew he would be unable to defeat the Union forces if they united, but believed he could defeat them individually. Lee's soldiers began marching toward Gordonsville on August 13.

Second Bull Run Campaign

Jackson and his troops had already been sent back to the Shenandoah Valley, and four days before Lee's men advanced, he fought a battle at Cedar Mountain, Virginia. This was the beginning of the Second Battle of Bull Run Campaign. Had the federal troops not been heavily outnumbered, they might have defeated the Confederate hero at Cedar Mountain. But they lost, and the way was clear for Lee to attack

Pope. If Pope had been allowed to maneuver with his army, he might have escaped the trap Lee had laid to defeat him. Halleck, however, ordered Pope to stay where he was, while McClellan took too long to bring his army to Washington.

Lee almost trapped Pope's army on August 19, but Pope saw what was coming and retreated from the Rapidan River to the Rappahannock River. On August 25, the day that U.S. Secretary of War Edwin Stanton ordered the enlistment of up to 5,000 African American soldiers to acts as "guards for plantations and settlements," Lee tried again. He sent Jackson marching around Pope's right flank with 24,000 soldiers. This was a gamble, since some of McClellan's troops had reached Pope. His army now outnumbered Lee's.

Pope knew that Jackson was on the march, but thought that Jackson was going to take up a defensive position in the Shenandoah Valley. Jackson, however, chose to attack a supply depot 20 miles (32 km) behind Pope's army on August 26.

Union Generals Outwitted

Pope realized that he was in danger of being surrounded. He left his defenses along the Rappahannock and marched back to Manassas Junction. Pope, with his larger army, now tried to catch Jackson's forces. Late on August 28, near the Bull Run battlefield of the previous year, Pope's forces ran into Jackson's. Pope decided to take the initiative and planned to attack the next day.

However, Pope was so worried about Jackson that he seems to have forgotten about Lee who was rushing toward Jackson. On August 29, as Pope attacked Jackson, Lee was heading north. When one of Pope's corps commanders sighted a dust cloud south of Bull Run, he realized it was Lee and refused to attack Jackson.

The Union commander was right, but the Confederates did not attack that day. They waited until August 30. Pope began the day with another attempt to smash through Jackson's defenses, which included part of an embankment. Jackson's men ran short of ammunition and threw rocks at the Union forces.

General Stonewall Jackson (center), one of the South's key generals. His superior, Robert E. Lee, owed many of his successes to Jackson's ability to move his forces at speed and then deploy them where they would have the most impact.

LEE'S INVASION OF THE NORTH

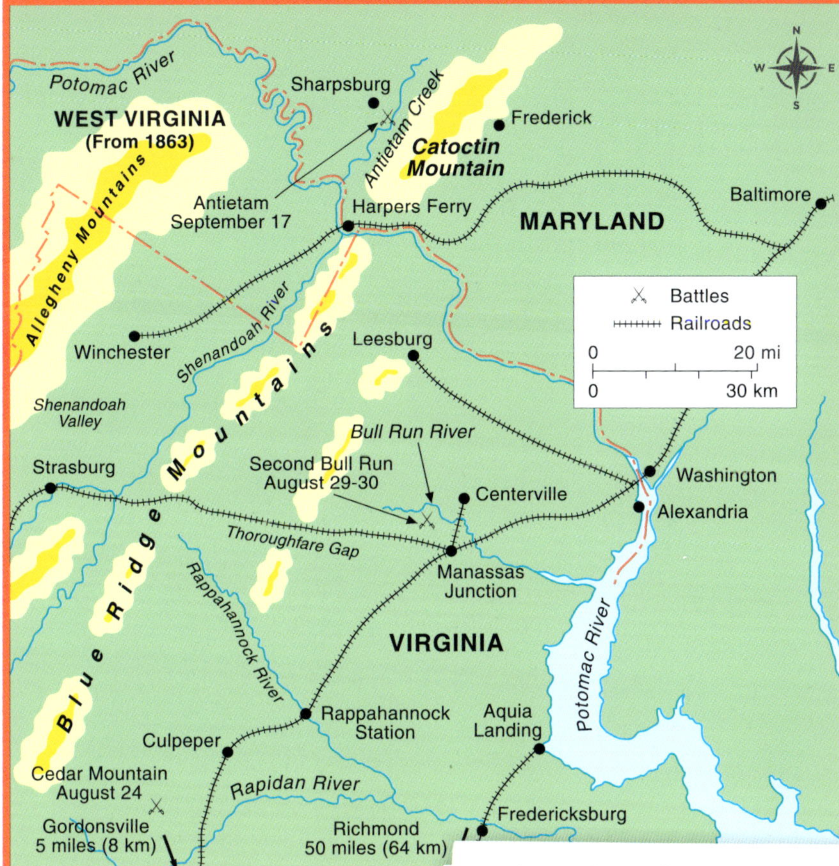

In 1862 the South's General Robert E. Lee devised a bold strategy to invade the North with the aim of capturing Washington, D.C. His plan came close to success but he was forced to retreat after the Battle of Antietam, fought on September 17.

Jackson's men hung on to the embankment. Then Lee unleashed his troops on one of the flanks of the federal forces. Pope was forced to retreat.

Lee now believed that the Confederacy had a chance to win the war. There were elections to Congress in the fall and many politicians in the North opposed the war. A victory in Maryland or Pennsylvania—close to Washington—might help these men. Lincoln might have to consider peace negotiations. Lee led his army into Maryland.

The Battle of Antietam

Lincoln now called McClellan back into command, and McClellan had a piece of good luck. On September 13 his soldiers found Lee's plans in a field. McClellan knew exactly where he could attack Lee with the best chance of success. However, as in

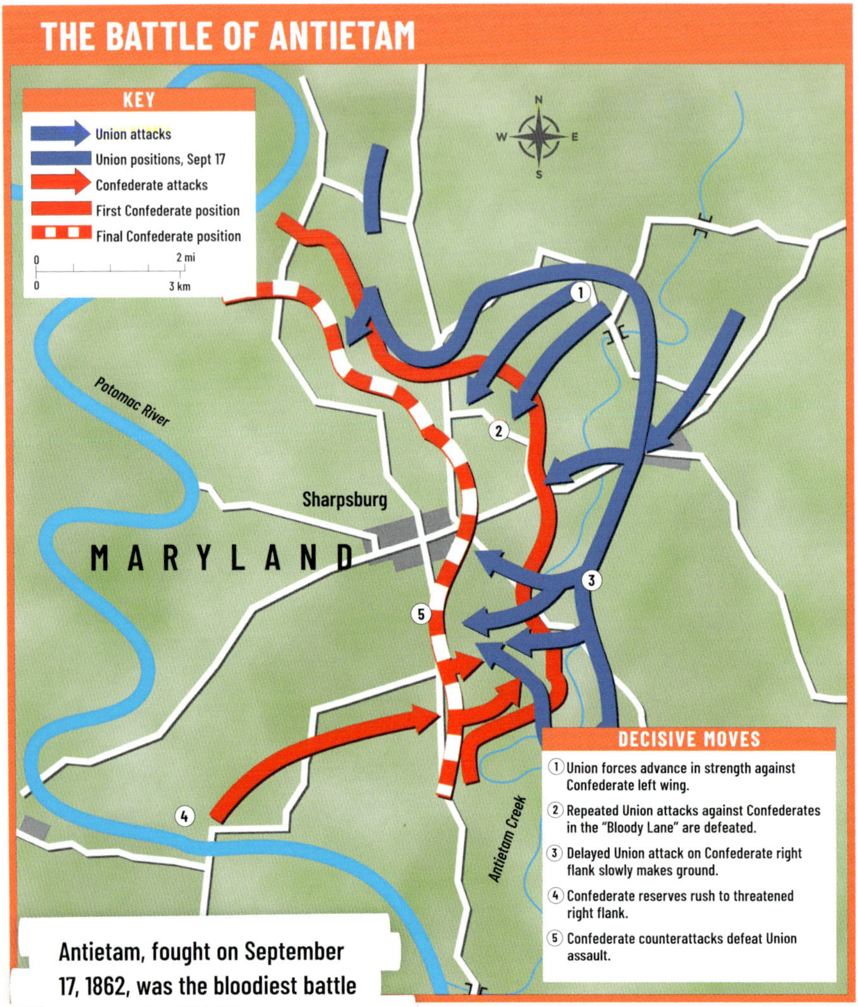

Antietam, fought on September 17, 1862, was the bloodiest battle of the entire Civil War.

the past, McClellan was so slow in moving his army that Lee could see where he was going to be attacked. The Union blow would fall along Antietam Creek, near Sharpsburg, Maryland, where there was a division of Southern troops. Lee began to assemble his Army of Northern Virginia—50,000 troops—there.

McClellan's large army arrived late on September 15 but he did not attack until the 17th. If the three Union corps he used had struck all at once, the Confederate army would have been overwhelmed. However, they attacked separately. Lee was always able to find some troops to reinforce the most endangered part of his line. The fighting began at dawn and did not end until dusk. When it was over, it had claimed more American lives in combat than any other day in our history—more than 23,000 men were killed or wounded in total. Many had died fighting over

THE EMANCIPATION PROCLAMATION

When Robert E. Lee invaded Maryland, President Lincoln made what he was reported as calling a promise with God. If the Confederate invasion of the North was defeated, Lincoln would issue an emancipation proclamation to free all enslaved people in Confederate-held territory.

On September 22, 1862, four days after the Union victory at the Battle of Antietam, Lincoln issued a preliminary proclamation stating that he would free enslaved people in the Confederacy on January 1, 1863, unless the Confederates returned to the Union. Afterward Lincoln came under pressure from politicians opposed to ending slavery. He had always said in the past that the war was to restore the Union, not end slavery. But Lincoln hated slavery.

As the war continued, he sided with the views of radical Republicans, who wanted to free all enslaved people right away. Lincoln believed he had given slaveholders in the seceded Southern states who wanted to restore the Union every chance. On January 1, 1863, he kept his promise and issued the Emancipation Proclamation.

a sunken road, which became known as "Bloody Lane."

Lee retreated, so McClellan could claim he had won. But Lincoln believed, rightly, that McClellan's slowness in following Lee had cost him an even greater victory. In November, McClellan was removed. Lincoln, however, did use the "victory" at Antietam to make clear his intention to issue his Emancipation Proclamation, the document that was to end slavery in the United States.

The charge of the Union "Iron Brigade" in the morning of the Battle of Antietam that threatened Stonewall Jackson's position near Dunker Church.

The First Campaigns of Grant

The eastern theater of operations, particularly the area between Washington and the Southern capital Richmond, was seen by the leaders of both sides as the key battleground in the Civil War. But the first great Union victories came in the west. In 1862, a previously undistinguished general, Ulysses S. Grant, displayed the fighting qualities that were lacking in many other Union commanders. In hard fighting he took the offensive against the seceded Southern states and by the end of the year had put the Union in a strategically superior position in the Mississippi valley, threatening to cut the Confederacy in two.

In July 1861 Kentucky was probably the most important state of the United States. Although many of its people were pro-Confederate, they did not want a war. Kentucky's governor and state legislature did not want to openly take sides between the Union and the Confederate states. They had proclaimed their wish for neutrality and hoped that both sides would respect their views.

The Confederates were the first to ignore the Kentuckians' appeal.

The bombardment of Fort Henry by Union gunboats under the command of Andrew Foote. The fall of Fort Henry in February 1862 was the first success of forces under the command of Ulysses S. Grant. Later that month Grant and Foote moved swiftly on to take Fort Donelson.

GRANT'S FIRST VICTORIES

The Civil War was going badly for the Union in the first months of 1862 except in the western theater of operations. Much of the fighting centered on the Mississippi River and its tributaries. One Northern commander, General Ulysses S. Grant, showed the drive and imagination needed to defeat the Southern forces based in the region.

In September Southern soldiers occupied the town of Columbus, Kentucky, and placed some of their artillery on high ground overlooking the Mississippi River. Union ships attempting to sail south down the Mississippi would be within range and could be bombarded and sunk by these artillery batteries.

In response the federal commander at Cairo, Illinois, General Ulysses S. Grant, occupied the town of Paducah, Kentucky, in November. This move demonstrated Grant's genius. While it was true that any army holding Columbus controlled the Mississippi, it was also true that an army holding Paducah controlled whoever held

The Second Iowa Regiment attacks Confederate positions at Fort Donelson in February 1862. Union troops proved resolute in the engagements around Fort Donelson and stopped an attempted breakout by the Confederates.

Columbus. From Paducah a force could travel down the Tennessee River and cut Columbus off from the Confederacy.

Attacking Fort Henry

Grant was already on the move by the time the Confederate commander, Albert Sydney Johnston, realized the danger. At the end of January 1862 a U.S. naval officer, Andrew Foote, took a force of soldiers and gunboats to attack the Confederate-held Fort Henry on the Tennessee River. On February 6, Foote surrounded the fort and bombarded it into surrendering.

On neighboring Cumberland River was another Confederate post—Fort Donelson. Johnston sent a large part of his army there to reinforce it after he learned of Grant's advance down the Tennessee. With these reinforcements Fort Donelson was defended by 15,000 Confederate troops. Foote sailed his gunboats back up the Tennessee to the Ohio River, and then down the Cumberland. Meanwhile, Grant marched overland.

Fort Donelson Falls

Grant and Foote reached Donelson, Tennessee, on February 12. Grant's troops surrounded the Confederate fort. Federal gunboats prepared to attack from the Cumberland River. On the 13th, federal troops attacked the fort, and on the 14th, the Union vessels opened fire. The boats sailed close to the shore and several were damaged by Confederate guns. The Confederate defenders of Fort Donelson were delighted. They had believed that the Union gunboats would bombard them into surrendering. Now they believed they had a chance of winning.

The three Confederate generals—John Floyd, Gideon Pillow, and Simon Bolivar Buckner—decided to try to break out of the federal trap.

A 200-pounder Parrott gun, often called a Parrot rifle. This U.S.-designed gun was used both in the field and during sieges. It was highly accurate and could hit specific targets at long range.

They attacked one part of the federal army besieging them just before dawn on February 15. Grant was away conferring with Foote, so the federal defenses were not ready. However, the Confederates were unable to break through. Floyd and Pillow escaped with some of their men on the night of February 15, but Buckner and the rest surrendered the following day.

"Unconditional Surrender!"

When the Confederates asked for surrender terms, Grant replied that "no terms except an unconditional and immediate surrender can be accepted." Some 16,500 Confederate soldiers surrendered. The North had a much-needed victory and Grant won a nickname—"Unconditional Surrender" Grant.

A week later Johnston abandoned Nashville, Tennessee. He had been forced out of Kentucky by Grant's advance on Fort Henry, and now he lost northwest Tennessee as well. Another federal force, the Army of the Ohio, advanced from Cincinnati, Ohio, through Bowling Green, Kentucky, to Nashville. Federal troops occupied the Tennessee state capital on February 24, 1862. The future also looked bleak for the Confederates elsewhere. On March 8 their last attempt to take over Missouri failed at the Battle of Pea Ridge in northwestern Arkansas. The Union commander of the Mississippi area, Henry Halleck, was slow to make use of his advantages, however. He found it difficult to coordinate the movements of three armies.

Marching to Shiloh

The key was Grant's Army of the Tennessee, advancing along that river toward Corinth, Mississippi, an important road and rail junction. On Grant's left was the Army of the Ohio commanded by General Don Carlos Buell; on his right, an army commanded by John Pope was trying to capture Confederate forts along the Mississippi. Johnston realized that by beating Grant, it might be possible then to turn on Buell and Pope. All available Confederate soldiers in the area were assembled at Corinth. In early April they marched the 30 miles (48 km) toward Grant at Shiloh Church in Tennessee.

The federal commanders at Shiloh did not believe that Johnston was going to attack them. So Johnston's soldiers came through the woods surrounding the federal camps at Shiloh on April 6 and found an enemy unready for battle. Many federal soldiers fled as the Southern troops charged from the woods, pausing briefly to fire a volley before resuming their remorseless advance.

The Hornet's Nest

Grant's army held in two places, which was of vital importance. General William Tecumseh Sherman resisted for a time on Grant's left, while in the center the "Hornet's Nest" was held by troops commanded by General Benjamin Prentiss. This position gained its name because the buzz of bullets fired at close range sounded like the noise made by hornets.

The fight for the Hornet's Nest gave Grant time to construct a new defensive line about three miles (5 km) back from the original front with almost all the army's artillery on its left. When the Confederates reached this spot, night was falling. Earlier in the day Johnston had been wounded twice and bled to death. He was succeeded by Pierre Beauregard, commander at Fort Sumter and Bull Run. The delay in changing command was crucial to the outcome of Shiloh. Beauregard decided to reorganize the army and attack the next morning.

Second Day at Shiloh

The Confederate leaders did not realize that Union reinforcements were arriving. Sherman met Grant that night. "We've had the devil's own day," he said. "Yes," Grant said,

Northern artillery fire on the Confederates at the Battle of Shiloh, April 6-7, 1862. Grant is shown mounted at right. Although Grant was able to force the Southern army to retreat, he was criticized for the heavy casualties he suffered. However, President Lincoln brushed aside demands for Grant to be fired saying: "I can't spare this man. He fights."

THE BATTLE OF HAMPTON ROADS

On March 8, 1862, a Confederate ship, the *Merrimack* (C.S.S. *Virginia*), sailed down the James River and attacked the U.S. Navy squadron in Hampton Roads off the coast of Virginia. The Confederates had covered most of the ship above the waterline in an iron shell and cannons poked through its sides. The *Merrimack's* armor was so strong that it could not be penetrated by cannonballs. Two Union wooden warships, the *Cumberland* and *Congress*, were sunk because the *Merrimack* could fire on and ram them without danger. The *Merrimack* planned to return the next day to sink more vessels.

Overnight, however, the U.S. Navy's own ironclad, the U.S.S. *Monitor*, arrived in Hampton Roads. While the *Merrimack* was described as "a half-submerged barn" because of its shape, the *Monitor* was called "a tin can on a shingle" because it had a revolving turret, which was placed in the middle of a flat hull that was barely above the water.

When the *Merrimack* came out to fight on March 9, the two ironclads battled all morning. They damaged one another slightly, but neither's guns could do any important damage because of the thickness of their armor. The *Monitor* did prevent the *Merrimack* from sinking any more Union warships, however.

The Battle of Hampton Roads was the first combat between ironclad ships in history. Neither vessel survived the war. The *Merrimack* was burned to avoid capture in May 1862, while the *Monitor* sank in high seas on December 31, 1862.

"We'll lick 'em tomorrow, though." The federal troops did exactly that. They surprised the Confederates on April 7. Beauregard saw that he was outnumbered, and his army retreated to Corinth, Mississippi. Shiloh was a federal victory but was costly. The South suffered 10,500 casualties, but Grant had even more, about 13,000. Halleck came to take command of both Grant's and Buell's armies for the attack on Corinth.

Taking New Orleans

The same day that Beauregard retreated from the Shiloh battlefield, an important Confederate stronghold on the Mississippi River, Island Number Ten, surrendered to Pope's army. Three weeks later, on the night of April 24–25, a federal fleet led by David Farragut defeated the Confederates at New Orleans, Louisiana. The city was occupied by federal troops on April 29.

During May Halleck moved on Corinth, which Beauregard abandoned on May 29. Beauregard was removed from command of the main Confederate army, then at Tupelo, Mississippi.

Memphis, Tennessee, fell to federal forces on June 6, and the only remaining Confederate-controlled city between New Orleans and Memphis was Vicksburg. It seemed that victory for the Union in the western theater of operations was near. The South was very close to being split in two.

The federal commanders, however, failed to take full advantage of the situation. Buell tried to take Chattanooga, Tennessee, but moved so slowly that the Confederate general at Tupelo in northern Mississippi, Braxton Bragg, was able to get 30,000 of his soldiers there first.

Bragg moved his troops by railroad, one of the first such strategic movements in military history. Then Bragg marched north to Kentucky and Buell had to retreat in order to protect his lines of supply. On October 8, at Perryville, the two armies fought a drawn battle, but Bragg had to retreat since he was far from his base at Chattanooga, while Buell was very close to his base at Cincinnati, Ohio.

Confederate general Braxton Bragg. He ordered an attack on Union forces at Murfreesboro in January 1863 that was a costly defeat for the Confederacy.

Grant Moves on Vicksburg

All summer Grant had been unhappy. He was in command of the Union forces that were holding west Tennessee and not of those fighting the Confederates directly. Grant watched the war develop and had a clear idea of what he wanted to do. First, he had to repel an attack on his advanced forces at Iuka, Mississippi, by Southern soldiers from Arkansas. These Confederates later assaulted Corinth, Mississippi, on October 3, where they were beaten off by General William S. Rosecrans's Union troops.

Rosecrans's success earned him a promotion. Buell was removed from command of the Army of the Cumberland and Rosecrans was appointed in his place. Grant, meanwhile, had to wait until November before he could resume his offensive. He moved against Vicksburg but he did not get very far before he had to halt. Halleck wanted a combined army and navy expedition to go down the Mississippi from Memphis to help Grant. Grant had to wait until all the troops for this maneuver were in Memphis. This took a month. Grant then resumed his advance, with Sherman moving down the west bank of the Mississippi to assist the advance.

However, the delay allowed two large Confederate cavalry columns, one of 2,000 led by General Nathan Bedford Forrest and one of 3,500 led by General Earl Van Dorn, to get behind Grant's army. They destroyed railroad tracks and telegraph lines. Grant had to abandon his attack on Vicksburg to repair the damage. He could not get word to Sherman, who believed that Vicksburg's defenders would be watching Grant. Instead, they waited for Sherman in the swamps at Chickasaw Bluffs, Mississippi, just north of Vicksburg. When Sherman tried to capture the position on December 29, he found it too strong for him. Grant paused to reorganize.

Rosencrans Attacks Murfreesboro

As Grant paused, Rosecrans acted. Bragg and the Army of Tennessee were at Murfreesboro, Tennessee; Rosecrans was at nearby Nashville. Lincoln desperately prodded Rosecrans to act but Rosecrans waited until he had enough food before advancing. The day after Christmas Rosecrans began moving on Bragg's troops. Bragg's cavalry scouts alerted him that Rosecrans was near, so Bragg decided to attack first. When Rosecrans's army camped near Murfreesboro on December 30, Bragg readied an attack. He struck at dawn on New Year's Eve.

Bragg believed that Rosecrans would retreat. He had forced the federal army into a v-shape, with its back to Stones River. But Rosecrans still believed he could win. On January 1, 1863, both sides limited their fighting to skirmishing. On January 2, Bragg decided he would have to force the Union army to move by attacking. He ordered some of his troops to cross Stones River and attack federal forces that occupied a hill.

If the Confederates could capture the hill, they might force Rosecrans to retreat. However, Rosecrans had massed his artillery batteries to protect the troops on the hill. When Bragg's soldiers attacked, they were caught in a crossfire. The assault was a failure. Casualties at Murfreesboro were equal, about 12,000 per side, but it was a Union victory since Bragg had to retreat.

Turning the Tide

During 1862 the war in the western theater had largely favored the federal side. The Confederates had come close to defeating the Northern army, but they failed to inflict any defeat. Twice the Confederates nearly gained much-needed victories, at Shiloh and at Murfreesboro. It was the self-confidence of the federal commanders and their troops' steadfastness under fire that had defeated the Confederate forces.

The resources of the North were slowly turning the tide against the Confederacy. The Union forces were also being led by commanders who were skilled and knew how to use their troops to grind down the forces that opposed them. Attrition—the ability to wear down an enemy—and not bravery was becoming the deciding factor in both battles and campaigns.

From Fredericksburg to Gettysburg

In late 1862 and early 1863, Robert E. Lee won major victories against Union forces at Fredericksburg and Chancellorsville. In the wake of these successes he decided to march north into Pennsylvania and then strike south toward Washington. As in the previous year, he hoped that capturing the capital of the Union would bring the war to an end. In early July, his Confederate forces met a federal army at Gettysburg, sparking a three-day battle that would decide the fate of the Confederacy.

President Lincoln's replacement for General George McClellan as commander of the Army of the Potomac in November 1862, General Ambrose Burnside, had not wanted the job. He only agreed to it because he would otherwise have had to serve under General Joseph Hooker, whom he did not like at all. However, Burnside seemed to have the military knowledge and experience that were needed to fill the post. Burnside had scored

Union troops of Humphrey's Division advance toward Marye's Heights at the Battle of Fredericksburg, December, 1862.

PRISONERS OF WAR

Until the spring of 1862 neither Union nor Confederate armies thought much about looking after prisoners of war. If people were captured, commanders in the area would often work out an agreement to exchange them. But after the fall of Fort Donelson in February 1862, the number of prisoners captured by both sides increased rapidly.

In July 1862 the Union and Confederate armies agreed to a system of exchanging prisoners that lasted until the Confederates began to capture African American soldiers. These soldiers were shot, or sold into slavery, or put in jail. The Union authorities, therefore, stopped all prisoner exchanges.

Soldiers now began to be kept in camps. These could be old forts, but some were little more than a wooden stockade surrounding an open field. Andersonville, a Confederate prison, was the worst of these camps. Tens of thousands of Union soldiers died there through disease, starvation, and poor treatment. Its commander, Henry Wirz, was hanged after the war.

important victories in several landings along the North Carolina coast. Forces under his command had captured the Confederate bases at Roanoke Island, New Berne, and Beaufort during February and March 1862.

Burnside's career as commander of the Army of the Potomac seemed to have gotten off to a good start. The action took place in Virginia. Lee was near Manassas, and Burnside simply marched to the town of Fredericksburg. Burnside was now closer to Richmond than Lee was. The only problem was that there were many large rivers to cross on the way, the first being the Rappahannock. These crossings would slow Burnside down, giving Lee time to catch up with him.

Bloody Disaster

Burnside called himself a fighting general, but anyone writing about him would have to say he was an unlucky general, first and foremost. Having gained a march on Lee, Burnside was then kept waiting for some pontoons—floating barges—that would allow him to build bridges across the Rappahannock. By the time they arrived, so had Lee. The Confederates occupied some hills above the town. Lee believed Burnside had been outmaneuvered and would be forced to withdraw.

Lee's position at Fredericksburg was too strong for Burnside to attack. Burnside, however, stuck to his plans. On December 13, the Union army attacked. It was a bloody repulse. Out of 100,000 federal soldiers in the Army of the Potomac, 15,000 were killed or wounded. Lincoln said that "the country cannot endure such losses." The Army of the Potomac fell back from Fredericksburg.

When Burnside attempted to resume his campaign against

Richmond in January 1863, he had more bad luck. After a month of dry weather, just as he began to move, heavy rain turned the roads to mud.

Some of Burnside's officers had complained to Lincoln about his leadership. Burnside now went to Lincoln with a list of generals he wanted removed. Either they would go, or Burnside would. Since the generals Burnside wanted to remove were protected by powerful politicians, and Burnside had not defeated Lee, Lincoln got rid of Burnside. Lincoln made General Joseph Hooker, a man who drank a lot of alcohol and did a lot of bragging, the new commander of the Army of the Potomac. Hooker also boasted frequently about what a great military commander he was. Now Lincoln decided to take him at his word.

Throughout the spring of 1863 both Hooker's and Lee's armies remained inactive. The heavy rains continued, making it hard to move. Both armies, however, were also in no shape to attack. The federal army had been poorly supplied under Burnside and few men received leaves. Hooker changed this, which raised morale. He also held military parades with flags and music that helped make his troops feel more like soldiers. Lee's troops were very confident because of their recent victories, but they lacked shoes or food. The railroads in Virginia were running very badly, and although there was food in the Confederacy that could have been given to the Army of Northern Virginia, there was no way to get it there. Food shortages would, sooner or later, force Lee to move.

Chancellorsville: Lee's Greatest Victory

Hooker's army numbered about 120,000, twice the number of soldiers that Lee had. Lee was still

A key moment at the Battle of Chancellorsville. "Stonewall" Jackson is fatally wounded after leading his men on the flanking march that won the fight for the Confederates. He was a major loss.

THE SHARPS CARBINE

Loading a rifled musket (a gun with spiral grooves cut into the barrel) in 1861 was a difficult task. The bullet had to be loaded from the muzzle, or top, of the gun's barrel. Gun designers realized that to load the bullet in the breech, or bottom, of the barrel would allow more rapid shooting.

A gunsmith named Christian Sharps came up with one method of breechloading. The hammer would be pulled back, and a lever would open the breech of the barrel up like a trapdoor. The bullet and black powder cartridge would then be put into the breech, which would be pushed shut. The Sharps carbine did not have the same range as a rifle, but it did have a higher rate of fire. It was also more expensive to make than other weapons, since the trapdoor mechanism was complex. Some other breechloaders had magazines (cartridge holders) containing seven or more bullets. A lever that was moved after firing placed a new bullet in the breech. But these complicated weapons were even more expensive than the Sharps. Almost 90,000 Sharps carbines were manufactured.

The Sharps carbine saw considerable service during the Civil War, mainly with the Union forces. It was chiefly used by Northern cavalry regiments.

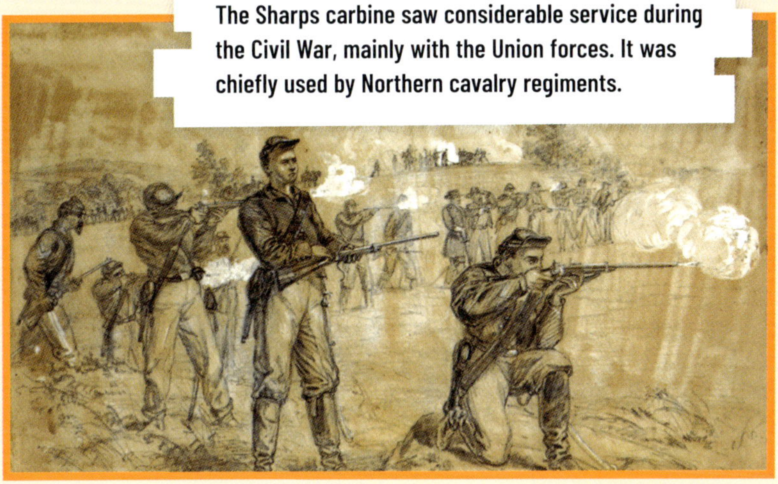

in his strong defensive position at Fredericksburg, where he had beaten Burnside. Hooker knew he was unlikely to win if he attacked Lee directly, so he decided to force him out of his defenses by marching around his flank.

At the end of April 1863, Hooker led some 75,000 of his army west along the Rappahannock, and crossed the river. He then entered an area of dense forest called the Virginia Wilderness. Meanwhile, Hooker left about 47,000 soldiers at Fredericksburg. Lee had just over 50,000. If Lee attacked the Union forces Hooker had left at Fredericksburg, Hooker, with the main army, would strike at the Confederate rear. If Lee attacked

THE CHANCELLORSVILLE CAMPAIGN

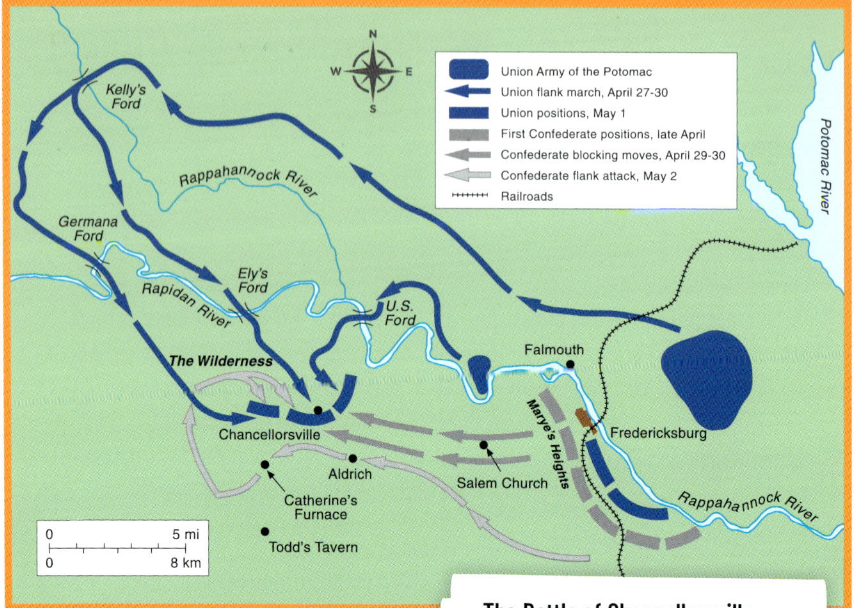

The Battle of Chancellorsville was Lee's most brilliant battle. Although outnumbered, he moved with lightning speed against larger Union forces and forced them to retreat after several days of heavy fighting.

Hooker's main army, the Union soldiers left at Fredericksburg would be able to strike at Lee's rear. Hooker believed that Lee was trapped between the two large Union forces.

Hooker's plan needed the larger Union force, in the Wilderness, to move quickly. On April 30, he halted his forces at the edge of the Wilderness near a village called Chancellorsville. His generals expected him to continue advancing into more open country where the larger size of the Army of the Potomac would give them a great advantage in battle. But Hooker refused to advance any farther. All his bragging hid a lack of self-confidence. Once in command, at the point when he needed to be confident, Hooker was not. He had advanced into a position where he threatened Lee's army, hoping that Lee would retreat. Lee, however, wanted to fight, although he was outnumbered.

Lee also divided his army. He left 10,000 men commanded by General Jubal Early at Fredericksburg, and took the rest to the Wilderness. When he learned that Hooker had halted, Lee divided his army again. On May 2, "Stonewall" Jackson took 28,000 men around Hooker's right wing. When Jackson attacked, the Union soldiers were caught by surprise. Jackson's assault hit the corps commanded by General Oliver Otis Howard, while the Union

Pickett's Charge, the final desperate attack by Lee's Confederates at the Battle of Gettysburg.

soldiers were eating. They ran away.

Jackson now wanted to find a ford across the Rappahannock and cross it so that Hooker's army could not retreat back to Washington. Jackson went to look for the ford, but was accidentally shot by one of his own men while returning in the dusk. He died later. With the loss of this great general—"My right arm," said Lee—the Confederates had to regroup.

On May 3, the Confederates resumed their attack. Hooker was wounded. He was now more concerned with protecting his line of retreat than attacking Lee. By this stage the Union troops at Fredericksburg under General John Sedgwick had begun to move forward. Lee once again divided his army and halted Sedgwick's advance at Salem Church on May 4.

On May 5, Hooker withdrew across the Rappahannock. Lee used the advantage he had gained to invade the North once again.

Advance through Pennsylvania

During the first week of June 1863, Lee began marching from Fredericksburg into Pennsylvania. On the way his troops seized free African Americans and sent them back to Virginia to be enslaved. In contrast, Lincoln had recently given freed people assurances that they were to be permitted to serve in the army. Lincoln, instead of being alarmed at Lee's approach, was delighted. He believed that if Lee was defeated on federal territory many miles from his home bases, his army could be destroyed.

A Pennsylvanian, General George Gordon Meade, replaced Hooker on June 28. Hooker had resigned because a plan of his to trap Lee's army had been overruled by his superiors. Meade wanted to fight, and so did Lee. However, neither of them had intended to fight at Gettysburg, Pennsylvania.

The Battle Begins

On July 1, some Confederate soldiers approaching the town in search of shoes came under fire from federal cavalry. The battle gradually absorbed more and more of the two armies. When Lee arrived during the afternoon, he decided that he could at least defeat a part of the federal army. He ordered a general advance. The Union troops were in a rough semicircle around the town of Gettysburg.

The fighting raged on into the evening. The constant pressure of more and more Southern troops arriving caused the Union lines to collapse. General Oliver Howard's Eleventh Corps, whose soldiers were mostly German-Americans, broke at a critical moment. The Union soldiers retreated through Gettysburg to the high ground southeast of the town, taking up positions on Cemetery Hill and Culp's Hill.

The battle resumed the next day, July 2. Lee sent General James Longstreet's First Corps to attack Meade's left flank. The key to the Union line was a hill at its south end called Little Round Top. It was supposed to be defended by troops led by General Daniel Sickles. Sickles believed that he would find it easier to defend the ground in front of him. During the morning he occupied positions known as the Peach Orchard, the Wheatfield, and the Devil's Den (an area strewn with large boulders). However, the new positions exposed both his flanks to attack. By the time Sickles realized the danger, he was about to be attacked.

Lee's Army Retreats

Longstreet was very slow in coming to battle. He did not launch his attacks until the late afternoon. His men fought hard for the Wheatfield, the Peach Orchard, and Devil's Den. Sickles' men fought back hard. The Confederates gradually fought their way to Little Round Top. It looked as if the federal army would be outflanked. But Meade's chief of engineers, General Gouverneur Warren, got troops to Little Round Top just in time to stop Longstreet from capturing it.

On July 3, Lee sent his one fresh division, commanded by General George Pickett, together with two other divisions to attack the center of Cemetery Ridge. The assault by some 15,000 of Lee's best troops followed the biggest artillery bombardment yet seen in American history. About 150 of Pickett's men broke into the federal position, but many more had been killed or wounded. The survivors retreated. The Battle of Gettysburg was over. Meade had suffered about 23,000 men killed, wounded, and missing; Lee some 28,000 men.

On July 4, there was a thunderstorm that prevented Meade from attacking, and Lee began the retreat back to Virginia.

No one realized it but never again would Lee have any chance to win

THE BATTLE OF GETTYSBURG

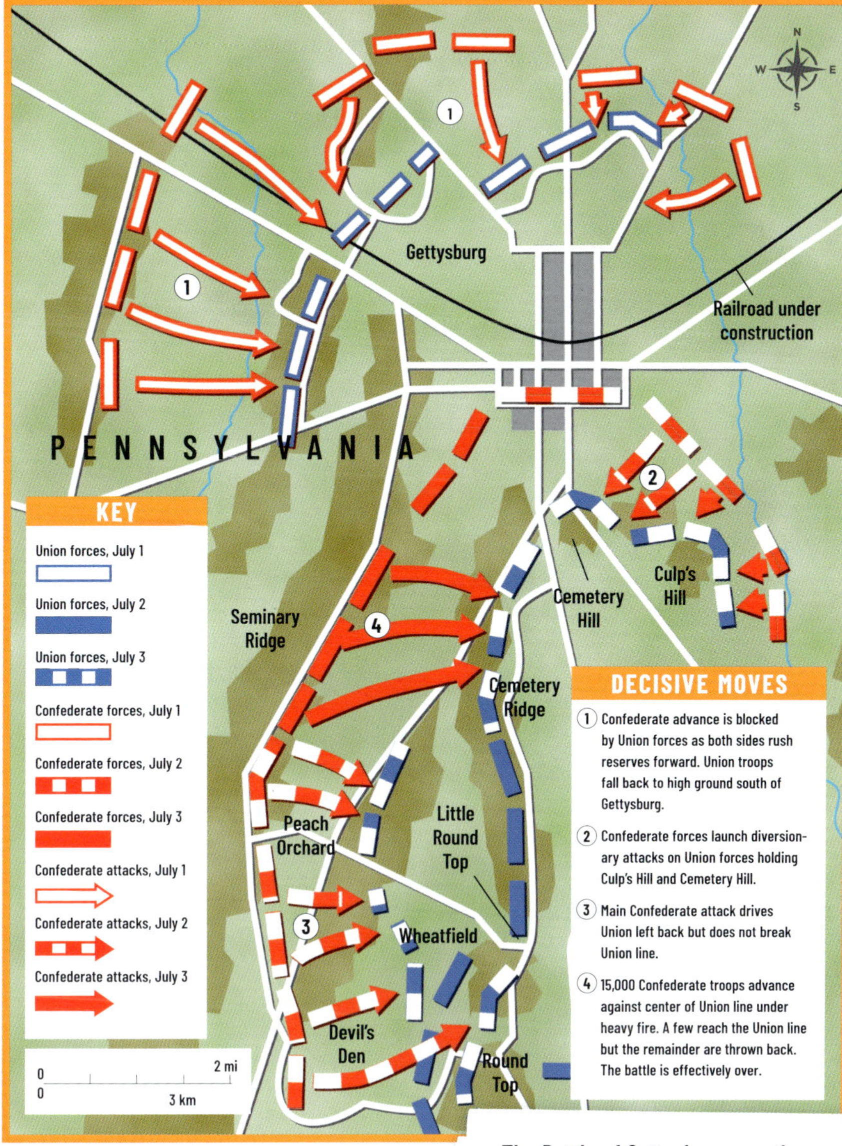

the war. The Battle of Gettysburg had torn the fighting heart out of the Army of Northern Virginia. Henceforth, Lee would fight battles to defend the Confederacy and not to win the war.

The Battle of Gettysburg was the decisive moment in the Civil War. Lee failed to defeat the Army of the Potomac and many of the most experienced soldiers in his Army of Northern Virginia were killed or wounded in the three days of fighting.

The Fall of Vicksburg

Union victories in 1862 had given the Confederate armies a problem in the west. But the seceded states still held the important strongpoint of Vicksburg on the Mississippi. Vicksburg was protected by the Mississippi itself and by steep bluffs rising from the river valley. Union commander General Grant came up with a bold plan, however. He prepared to sweep south and then cross the river to attack the city from the rear. It was a complex operation but capturing Vicksburg would split the Confederacy.

At the end of December 1862 all attempts by General Grant and his officers to reach Vicksburg had been unsuccessful. One of the worst setbacks for the Union had taken place in the previous July, when Admiral David Farragut's fleet failed to destroy a Confederate ironclad, the *Arkansas*, near Vicksburg, and fell back down the Mississippi to the coast.

The terrain around Vicksburg favored the defenders. Swamps blocked the way to Vicksburg from the north. The Mississippi was wide here, so Union troops could not cross from Arkansas easily—especially since Confederate guns could blast their boats.

Since the bulk of Grant's army was at Milliken's Bend northwest of Vicksburg, there was no way to get it east of Vicksburg except by heading north and crossing near Memphis, Tennessee, or by going south. To cross the Mississippi south of Vicksburg required gunboats and transport for the troops. But vessels could not easily sail past Vicksburg to connect with the Union troops that would march overland. Grant had already tried to get east of Vicksburg by marching from the north, but he had been forced to pull back because Confederate cavalry had attacked his supply lines.

River Strategy

Grant decided that somehow he would have to approach Vicksburg from the south. First, he tried to dig a canal. There was a bend in the Mississippi near Vicksburg. It made a kind of triangle with Vicksburg at one point. A canal should allow Grant's ships and gunboats to sail south past Vicksburg, but too far away for the Confederate artillery to shoot at them. Through January

Gunboats of Admiral David Porter's Union fleet sail past Vicksburg under intense artillery fire from the Southern artillery positioned on the bluffs overlooking the Mississippi River, April 1863.

and February of 1863 Grant's soldiers dug through swampy terrain. The winter weather did not help. Constant rain made the swampy ground even wetter. The soldiers were in danger of drowning. At the end of February Grant decided that his army was wasting its time. He then tried to sail some troops along the Yazoo River, which joined the Mississippi a little way north of Vicksburg. They could land just north of Vicksburg and advance on the city from that direction.

The Yazoo Narrows

However, the Yazoo was narrow, and swampy forests came right up to its banks. The boat commanders found that their vessels could not maneuver in the narrow channel and Confederate infantry from Vicksburg advanced to attack the vulnerable ships. It was easy for the Confederates to protect the narrow river from the Union boats. At the end of March Grant yet again had to give up. General John Pemberton, the Confederate commander in Vicksburg, believed he had won a great victory.

Confederate confidence was only short lived, however. On April 16–17, in the dark of night, Union Admiral David Porter succeeded in running 12 ships down the Mississippi past the Confederate guns at Vicksburg.

General Ulysses S. Grant. Grant showed great persistence at Vicksburg. He tried various ways of getting south of the fortress before Admiral Porter's gunboats managed to sail past it at night.

Grant marched his army south to meet Porter's fleet. On April 30, 1863, Grant's army was transported across the Mississippi River at Bruinsburg, 30 miles (48 km) south of Vicksburg in Mississippi.

Taking a Risk

Grant was taking a great risk. His army was now south of Vicksburg, and there was no easy way for it to get supplies from its base at Memphis. But Grant believed that his troops could take food from the farms and plantations of Mississippi as they marched back northward to attack Vicksburg from the east.

On May 1, Union Generals John McClernand and James B. McPherson defeated a Confederate force at Port Gibson, freeing its batteries at Grand Gulf for Grant's use as a base. Grant's next target was the Mississippi state capital, Jackson. If federal troops could capture the state capital, their rear would be secure while they moved on Vicksburg.

On to Vicksburg

Grant began his northeastward march on May 7. He was now at risk of being caught between two Confederate armies—General Joseph Johnston was moving from Tennessee toward Jackson, while Pemberton came out of Vicksburg.

Grant's troops reached Jackson in a week but found that Johnston had arrived the day before. Johnston had only 6,000 soldiers, however. Grant ordered an immediate offensive. The federal army, outnumbering the Confederates by four to one, swamped their entrenchments around Jackson, sending Johnston and his troops retreating eastward on May 14.

Grant now quickly turned his army westward and defeated Pemberton at the Battle of Champion's Hill on May 16. On May 18, the Union army arrived outside Vicksburg itself. Grant believed that a quick assault might capture Vicksburg and avoid a long siege. The following day Sherman's corps attacked the northern side of the

THE VICKSBURG CAMPAIGN

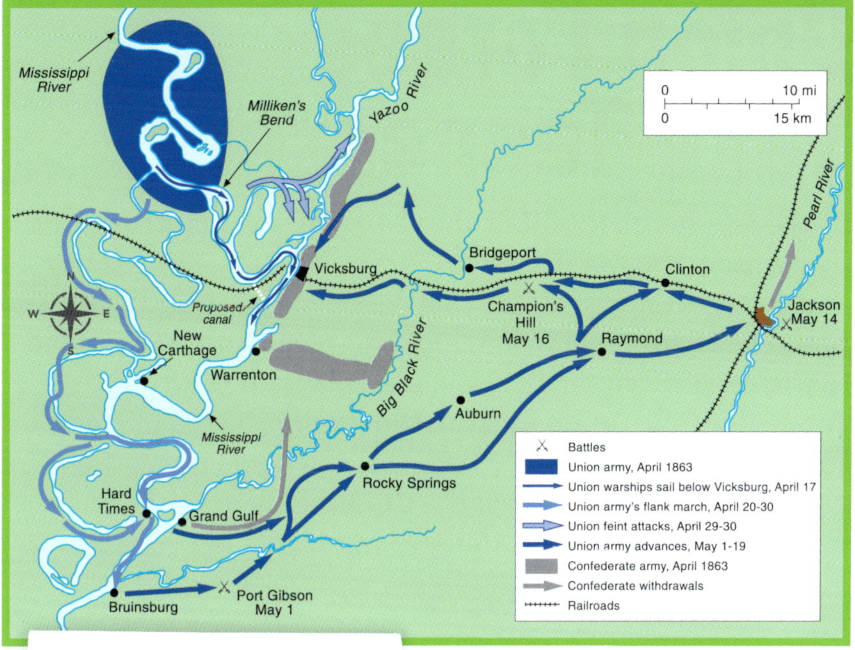

The key moment of the Vicksburg campaign came when Grant was able to position his army south of the city and then advance northward to launch an attack from the east on its Southern defenders.

city. It was driven off with the loss of 1,000 men. On May 22, the whole federal army attacked. Once again the Union assault troops suffered heavy losses.

Siege Warfare

Grant now recognized that he would have to besiege Vicksburg. He brought up guns and barges with mortars. For six weeks the city was hit by federal artillery. Pemberton watched his food supplies shrink. The gallant Confederate defenders were gradually being starved. The gunfire was so heavy that it drove the people of Vicksburg into caves.

On July 3, Pemberton asked Grant for terms of surrender. At first Grant said he wanted an unconditional surrender, but then he thought about it. To transport nearly 29,000 Confederate soldiers would take most of the riverboats he needed to keep his army supplied. He allowed Pemberton's men to be paroled—they could return home but had to give an oath that they would not fight again. On July 4, Vicksburg surrendered. Union control of the Mississippi River meant that the Confederacy was split in two. Grant also knew that Robert E. Lee had lost the Battle of Gettysburg the day before. The twin defeats doomed the Confederacy to defeat.

Union Forces Take Tennessee

By the late summer of 1863 the Confederacy was struggling to maintain the war. Ulysses S. Grant had taken Vicksburg and General George Meade had defeated Lee at Gettysburg. Now, President Lincoln and his senior commanders wanted to win decisive victories elsewhere, particularly in Tennessee. The Union Army of the Cumberland had made some progress, but Lincoln was looking for a large-scale victory. The commander of the Union army in Tennessee was replaced and a new offensive was begun late in 1863.

General William Rosecrans's Army of the Cumberland had won an important victory at Murfreesboro, Tennessee, (see map, page 31) in late December 1862 and January 1863. However, casualties had been so heavy that the Army of the Cumberland had to spend the entire spring of 1863 reorganizing. Rosecrans was worried that if he attacked the Confederate army of General Braxton Bragg, the Confederates would retreat toward Vicksburg and threaten Grant's efforts to capture their stronghold on the Mississippi.

Union Forces Reorganized

By the beginning of June Rosecrans was ready to advance.

General William Rosecrans led the Union's Army of the Cumberland from October 1862 until October 1863, when he was fired by General Grant.

BEDFORD FORREST'S RAIDS

Nathan Bedford Forrest had not attended any military academy when he became a Confederate cavalry officer. He was a wealthy slave trader and plantation owner who had paid for a whole battalion out of his private fortune. He was then elected its commander. He was trapped in Fort Donelson in February 1862, but escaped capture by breaking through the Union lines in a daring night maneuver.

Forrest became one of the key Confederate commanders of the war, always willing to try something new. His specialty was gathering large cavalry forces and leading them into the supply and communications network that spread out behind the Union armies.

He would tear down telegraph wires, rip up railroads, and burn federal supply dumps. His most important raid was against Grant in December 1862, which delayed the fall of Vicksburg.

However, Forrest had deeply racist opinions. He allowed African American prisoners to be killed and after the war was the first leader of the Ku Klux Klan.

By this time Bragg had managed to gather most of the harvest from the farms of central Tennessee, which provided some desperately needed wheat for the Confederacy. This, however, was the only success that Bragg would have that summer. Rosecrans at first wanted to attack Bragg in the middle of June, but his generals opposed his plans.

On June 24, however, Rosecrans took matters into his own hands and ordered an advance. Bragg's soldiers held many of the passes through the rugged terrain of the Cumberland Mountains. Rosecrans simply outflanked these defenses by moving a little farther east than Bragg expected. The Confederates abandoned western Tennessee to Rosecrans and retreated to Chattanooga.

On July 7, Rosecrans received a message from General Henry Halleck in Washington. Halleck pointed out that Grant had captured Vicksburg, and Meade had defeated Lee at Gettysburg. What could Rosecrans show for his spring offensive? Rosecrans wrote back. He said that, although his army had suffered just 570 casualties in its campaign, all of central Tennessee had been won from the Confederacy. It was a fair point, but Halleck and Lincoln only saw that Bragg's army still existed, while General John Pemberton's, which had been captured at Vicksburg, did not and Lee's Army of Northern Virginia was badly damaged due to the defeat at Gettysburg.

A Stroke of Bad Luck

Rosecrans remained at Murfreesboro for another six weeks. He used the time to gather supplies for his advance on his next target, Chattanooga, Tennessee. Rosecrans's army began to move in the middle of August. Confederate president Jefferson Davis in Richmond recognized the danger posed by Rosecrans. He decided to reinforce Bragg, taking troops from Virginia under General James Longstreet and sending them by railroad to Tennessee. Bragg waited until these troops arrived before making his attack. He had already worked out a careful plan.

Rosecrans occupied Chattanooga on September 6 and then moved south, heading toward Atlanta, Georgia. However, he marched with the corps of his army too widely separated to help each other if attacked. The biggest Union corps, commanded by General George Thomas, was in position at Chickamauga Creek, near the Georgia town of La Fayette. Bragg thought he could strike at the flank and front of this corps with a good chance of success.

Bragg suffered a stroke of bad luck. He first planned to attack on September 10, but the commanding officers of the Confederate corps refused, believing the plan was risky. Bragg tried again on the 11th, and once again his corps commanders objected to the plan. Thomas's exposed units now realized the danger and withdrew. Bragg tried attacking another Union corps, that of General John Crittenden, on the 13th. Again his commanders objected and no attack took place.

Thomas Stands Firm

The frustrated Bragg now waited six days before trying again. By this time many of Longstreet's troops had arrived in camp. Bragg's bad luck continued. Thomas reorganized his defenses the night before the attack, shifting his position so that Bragg's attack would hit part of his front, instead of his flank.

On the 19th, the Southern troops battered the Union left, where Thomas's corps was stationed. They gained very little. The terrain was heavily wooded, making

General George Henry Thomas showed great resolve at the Battle of Chickamauga in September 1863 and then led the troops of the Army of the Cumberland to a decisive victory at Missionary Ridge on November 25.

WAR IN THE WEST

In early 1862 General Henry Sibley, a Confederate, set out along the Rio Grande from Fort Bliss, Texas. He planned to invade California. In February he won a battle at Valverde, New Mexico. Sibley then captured Albuquerque and Santa Fe.

Sibley ran short of supplies and was forced to retreat. Union troops followed the Confederates and caught up with them south of Albuquerque, at Peralta. Sibley was driven back to Fort Bliss by May.

By early 1864 the Union was ready to invade Texas from Louisiana along the Red River. Command was given to General Nathaniel Banks, who was aided by a fleet under Admiral David Porter.

Porter was able to get a dozen of his gunboats past the rapids at Alexandria, Louisiana, and make for Shreveport. Banks headed overland to Shreveport by way of Grand Ecore. On April 8, he was attacked at Sabine Crossroads and forced to retreat to Alexandria. Porter also had to retreat. Alexandria was abandoned by the Union forces in May.

The last major action took place in late 1864, when a Confederate force was defeated at the Battle of Westport, Missouri, in October. The Confederates withdrew to Arkansas and then to Texas, ending the major fighting in the region.

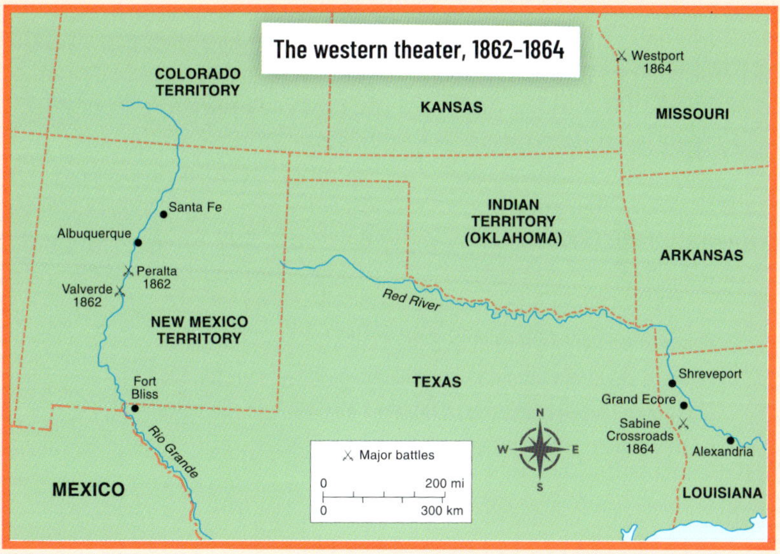

coordinated attacks almost impossible. That night Longstreet himself arrived with the rest of his corps. The attack resumed on the 20th. Once again the Confederates attacked and attacked, but gained little. Then Bragg received some compensation for his earlier bad luck. Rosecrans's staff had been reinforcing Thomas with troops from the right flank. But they lost track of what units were where.

They ordered one division to move closer to Thomas's position, not realizing that there was already a division there. The divisional commander, ordered to move, had to march around his neighbor. This created a huge hole in the line. Longstreet, coincidentally, launched a major attack at precisely this point.

The Rock of Chickamauga

The whole Union right ran back to Chattanooga. Thomas hung on until dusk, beating off every Southern assault. The fighting was hard. Then he retreated in good order to Chattanooga. For stemming the Confederates at the Battle of Chickamauga (see map, page 9), Thomas was nicknamed the "Rock of Chickamauga." Bragg had won a victory but with heavy losses. One-third of his 54,000 soldiers had been killed or wounded. He nevertheless followed Rosecrans and laid siege to Chattanooga.

By the middle of October Rosecrans's army was starving like the Confederate defenders of Vicksburg earlier that year. Lincoln ordered two corps from the Army of the Potomac west to help Rosecrans. He gave command of this force to General Joseph Hooker. At the same time William Tecumseh Sherman with four divisions was sent from Mississippi. General Ulysses. S. Grant was given command of all Union forces between the Appalachian Mountains and the Mississippi River. The reinforcements and the reorganization were to have a major impact on the campaign.

Grant Takes Charge

Grant moved his headquarters to Chattanooga (see map, page 9). He replaced Rosecrans with Thomas and studied the situation. He agreed to Rosecrans's plan to open a supply line from west of Chattanooga, which was accomplished on October 23. Then, on November 23, Grant began the Battle of Chattanooga. Hooker's troops climbed Lookout Mountain,

Union troops prepare to attack the Confederate defenses on Lookout Mountain outside Chattanooga on November 24, 1863. The Union forces managed to take the summit, but the main Confederate position remained intact.

Union troops from the Army of the Cumberland overwhelm the Confederates holding Missionary Ridge outside Chattanooga, Tennessee, on November 25, 1863.

a key position held by the Confederates that overlooked Chattanooga. The next day Hooker's troops swept the three brigades Bragg had placed there off the summit. Meanwhile, Sherman launched an attack on Bragg's right, but achieved only limited success. The Confederate positions there were stronger than anyone expected and Sherman's troops were still tired from marching to Chattanooga.

Missionary Ridge

On November 25 Grant asked Thomas to lead his Army of the Cumberland out of Chattanooga against Bragg's center at Missionary Ridge a little way to the south of Chattanooga and west of Lookout Mountain. Sherman would resume his attack on the Confederate left at the same time. The soldiers of the Army of the Cumberland were upset that they had not been trusted to attack the day before. They marched out of Chattanooga and across the fields between the town and the ridge determined to clear the Confederates off Missionary Ridge.

At the foot of the ridge there were Confederate soldiers in a line of trenches. The Union soldiers captured these, only to find that more Southern troops on the ridge above could shoot down at them. Then it was as if the whole of the attacking force became fired with anger. The Union troops stormed up the ridge despite heavy Confederate fire. As the Union soldiers got closer and closer to the Southern trenches above them, the Confederates were forced to retreat. Chattanooga was now securely in Union hands, and the Army of the Cumberland had avenged its defeat at the Battle of Chickamauga. Tennessee was finally clear of Confederate troops.

Grant's War of Attrition

Although President Lincoln hoped for swift victory over the South after the Battle at Gettysburg of July 1863, the generals he relied on were slow to continue the campaign against the Army of Northern Virginia under General Robert E. Lee. So, on March 2, 1864, Lincoln made General Ulysses S. Grant commander of all Union forces. Grant's plan for the year was simple. He would force Lee to fight at every opportunity. It was a recipe for heavy casualties but Grant knew that the South could not afford big losses in men.

General Grant photographed outside his tent. He saw that the Union would only win the Civil War by destroying the South's main army led by General Robert E. Lee.

After his defeat at the Battle of Gettysburg in July 1863, Lee got the major part of the Confederate Army of Northern Virginia back across the Potomac River into Virginia. General George Meade's failure to destroy Lee's army after Gettysburg made President Lincoln very angry as he believed, correctly, that Lee had escaped to fight another day.

The Union Army Attacks

On April 9, 1864, Grant, the new General-in-Chief of the Armies of the United States, gave Meade his orders for the new campaign: "Lee's army will be your objective point. Wherever Lee goes, there you will

GENERAL ULYSSES S. GRANT

Grant graduated from West Point in 1843. Two years later he took part in the Mexican-American War and fought bravely. But he had to resign from the army in 1854, after he took to drinking heavily while assigned to a lonely outpost on the West Coast. He was given an honorable discharge and went into business.

When the Civil War began in 1861, Grant felt he had been given a second chance. Thanks to the support of an ally of President Lincoln, Congressman Elihu Washburne, Grant was promoted and given a good command.

Grant's military method emphasized defeating the enemy army instead of capturing important towns or crossroads. He knew that the South could not continue to replace heavy losses. It was a simple but decisive strategy.

Grant became a national hero and even Lincoln was afraid Grant would run for president against him. Grant kept his political ambitions to himself until 1868, when he was elected to the White House. Grant served two terms as president and retired from public life in 1877.

go also." Grant planned to fight Lee's army to a standstill.

On May 4, Meade's Army of the Potomac marched south. It crossed the Rapidan River near the ford General Joseph Hooker had used on his way to his defeat at Chancellorsville in May 1863. Lee believed Grant had made a mistake. In the Wilderness, an area of dense forest with few roads, Lee saw that the superior numbers of the Union army would be less effective. Its advantage in artillery would be completely lost because artillery would not be able to move through the Wilderness's tangled undergrowth or be able to fire at anything other than very close range. He moved to attack Grant.

The Wilderness

The savage, confused Battle of the Wilderness (see map, page 9) began on May 5 and lasted for two days. Lee almost defeated Grant, but Southern general James Longstreet was badly wounded at a vital moment of the battle. The time spent reorganizing Longstreet's command cost the Confederates their victory.

Close Range Fighting

The Battle of the Wilderness was the most horrible of the whole Civil War. Many of the wounded of both sides died in agony, caught in the flames sparked by rifle and artillery fire that engulfed much of the tinder-dry undergrowth. Dense smoke clogged the battlefield and the battle hinged on which of the rival commanders acted boldly in the confusion. Grant was the first to act decisively. On May 7, he tried to get around Lee's right flank. The soldiers of the Army of the Potomac had expected to retreat after the mauling they had just suffered. They were surprised to find themselves still going forward.

Lee was also surprised by the Union response. He recognized that Grant's objective was the crossroads at Spotsylvania Courthouse. The race for the crossroads was won by the Confederates, who began digging trenches to form a salient—a strong U-shaped defensive position.

Heavy Union Casualties

Between May 10 and 12, Grant launched frequent attacks on Lee—at first small probing ones, then a whole corps was flung at the center of the Confederate salient. Maneuver was impossible. In one place 1,000 men confronted one another across the width of just 50 feet (15 m) in an area that became known as the "Bloody Angle." Close-range fire killed many. The dead were left in heaps. Grant's attacks slowly pushed Lee back, but still did not succeed in breaking through the Confederate front.

Cold Harbor

After a week in which both sides brought reinforcements from their rival capitals, Grant marched southeast again. He eventually attacked Lee at Cold Harbor, 10 miles (16 km) east of Richmond, where the Confederate troops waited behind earthen fortifications, in June. The Union soldiers believed the attack would

Union troops launch a bayonet charge against the Confederates during the Battle of Spotsylvania Courthouse, May 1864. The fighting was bitter and Grant was forced to admit failure when he was unable to cut through Lee's forces.

The Battle of Cold Harbor was a scene of carnage. Here, Union troops of the 7th New York Heavy Artillery, fighting as infantry, prepare to attack the Confederates. General Grant admitted in his memoirs that he regretted the frontal attacks in this battle, which led to enormous Union casualties against strong defenses.

fail. Hundreds took pieces of paper, wrote their names, and pinned them to their uniforms. This would allow their dead bodies to be easily identified and returned home for burial. Many did indeed die on June 3 in an attack on Lee's center that once again failed to break through well-sited Confederate defenses.

Losses That Could Not Be Replaced

Grant had lost over 50,000 soldiers in a month of almost continuous fighting. It was the highest casualty rate in the war. Lee had lost about half that many. But Grant had started with an army of 120,000. Lee had 64,000. Grant was proving to Lee that if the South did not surrender, he was prepared to lose half his army to kill every one of Lee's soldiers. Lee knew that the Confederacy could not stand to lose soldiers at this rate.

Jeb Stuart's Death

The Confederate casualty figures did not only include the rank and file. Senior commanders were also victims. "Stonewall" Jackson had already died at the Battle of Chancellorsville. Now, one of Lee's best commanders, Longstreet, was wounded in May. To complete a bad couple of months for the South, General Jeb Stuart, Lee's cavalry commander, was wounded in a clash with Union cavalry led by General Philip Sheridan at the Battle of Yellow Tavern, Virginia, on May 11 and died the next day.

Moving Toward Richmond

By the second half of 1864 the Confederacy was sliding to defeat. Starved of food, manpower, and weapons, its armies were facing much larger Union forces that were slowly converging on Richmond, the Southern capital. General Robert E. Lee knew that he lacked the resources to attack and so resorted to defensive warfare. The advance of the Northern armies centered on the communications center of Petersburg. The siege of Petersburg was one of the bloodiest events of the war.

When Grant led the Army of the Potomac into the Wilderness in May 1864, it was only one of three Union offensives that sought to drive the Confederate armies out of Virginia. The other two were a drive down the Shenandoah Valley and an assault along the James River north to Richmond. The Shenandoah attack was to capture the city of Staunton, but only got as far as the town of New Market. This

A Union mortar emplacement during the siege of the Southern city of Petersburg. The city finally fell in early April 1865.

Union advance was halted on May 15.

More hope was placed in the attack up the James River. This copied General George McClellan's move on Richmond in 1862, but the army this time was much smaller. General Benjamin Butler commanded only 30,000 soldiers. When he arrived at the village of Bermuda Hundred, the Union base between the James and Appomattox Rivers, there were just 10,000 Confederate soldiers around Richmond. Only a few of them were between Butler's army and the Southern capital. If Butler had moved up the banks of the James, he could have captured Petersburg, which was a key crossroads and railroad junction.

A Slow Advance

Butler's slowness gave the Southern commander, General Pierre Beauregard, time to gather reinforcements. At the Battle of Drewry's Bluff on May 16, Beauregard's soldiers attacked and forced Butler back to Bermuda Hundred. Butler was secure from attack behind his line of trenches, but was trapped.

ON TO RICHMOND

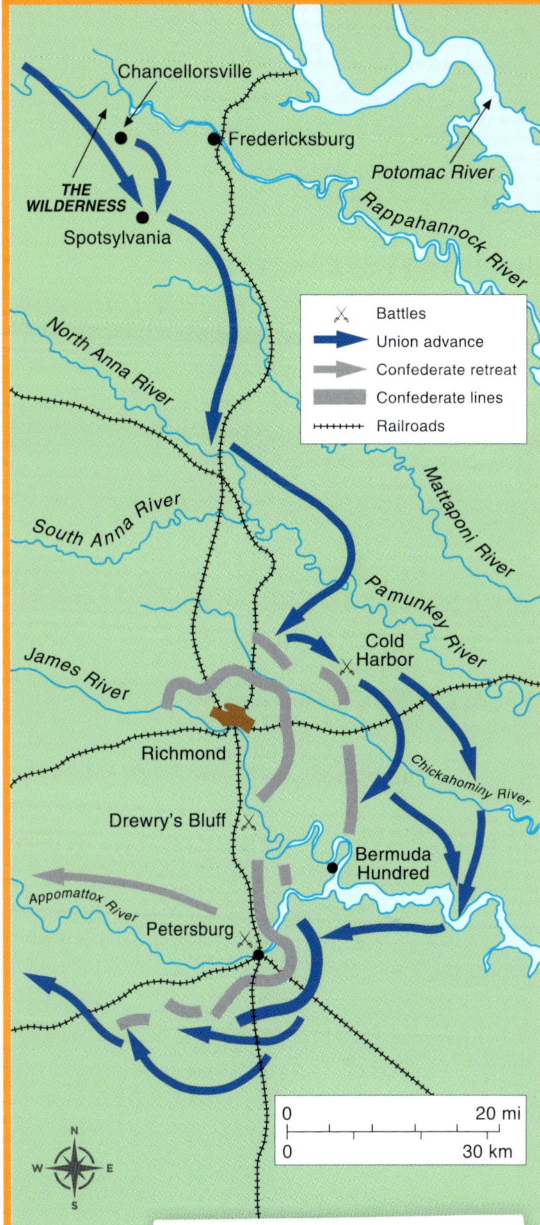

The Union campaign to capture Richmond in 1864 involved great sweeping movements around to the east and south of the Southern capital.

Butler's one achievement was to place an army near Richmond. After Grant's succession of attacks from the Wilderness to Cold Harbor had failed to destroy Lee's army, Butler's location became important. Grant decided on another three-pronged plan of attack.

Sheridan's Cavalry Army

The Union army in the Shenandoah would try once again to advance south. At the same time a large number of the Army of the Potomac's cavalry, commanded by General Philip Sheridan, would ride west to the Shenandoah. Sheridan's command would destroy railroads as it went. Sheridan and the Shenandoah force would stop food from getting to Lee. Without food, his army would starve.

Grant would take the Army of the Potomac, the third prong, across the James River close to where Butler's army was holed up and capture Petersburg. The Army of the Potomac began marching on June 12. One of the longest pontoon bridges in history was built across the James River, and on June 14 the bulk of Grant's army crossed. On June 15, Grant's leading corps neared Petersburg. It numbered about 15,000 soldiers. Only 2,000 Confederates, commanded by Beauregard, defended the isolated Virginia city.

A Missed Opportunity

For the next three days, the Union army could just about have marched into Petersburg without fighting. But the Union commanders botched the job, allowing the Confederates to rush reinforcements to the threatened city. By the time Grant arrived with another 65,000 Union soldiers, so had Lee.

Grant tried a final assault on June 18, with an attack by the whole of the Army of the Potomac. They found that Lee and Beauregard had moved their troops out of their trench line and fallen back closer to the city. Instead of continuing on, the Union soldiers halted. George Meade, commander of the Army of the Potomac, and Grant agreed to besiege Petersburg.

The Siege of Petersburg

For eight months the Union and Confederate armies sparred along the trench lines of Petersburg. There was one spectacular assault at the end of July 1864, which produced the Union defeat. Union engineers had tunneled under the Confederate lines and, on the 30th, detonated huge quantities of explosives. Originally, the Union Ninth Corps, an African American unit, had been earmarked to lead the assault but the orders were changed at the last minute. However, the detonation caught the Confederates by surprise and a huge gap appeared in their lines.

The Union troops supposed to exploit this advantage became stuck in the crater caused by the explosion. The Union assault troops, including many African Americans from the corps originally scheduled to lead the attack who were rushed forward to support the faltering advance, were fired on at close range by

General Philip Sheridan. He won the Battle of Cedar Creek on October 19, 1864. This victory over General Jubal Early cleared the Shenandoah Valley of Confederate forces late in 1864 .

the Confederates, who had recovered from their shock.

Despite showing great bravery, the Union troops failed to take advantage of the confusion caused by the explosion and nearly 4,000 became casualties. After this setback Grant attempted to cut the roads and railroads leading into Petersburg in the hope that Lee would retreat or surrender.

In October Grant finally gained total control of the Shenandoah Valley. The Union army there had been outmaneuvered on June 18. This allowed the Southern army, commanded by General Jubal Early, to march on Washington. The nation's capital might have fallen but Grant sent reinforcements, causing Early to retreat to the Shenandoah Valley. Grant also sent General Philip Sheridan after Early. Sheridan defeated Early. The final victory came at Cedar Creek (see map, page 9) on October 19. With the Shenandoah in Union hands, Lee lost his main food source.

Lee Quits Petersburg

Through the winter months of 1864–1865, Lee's army began to shrink. Lee's previously loyal soldiers now began to desert in large numbers. Metal to make bullets was in short supply, and the remaining Confederate soldiers were limited to firing no more than 18 shots in one day. Lee did not have enough troops to hold the 35 miles (56 km) of trenches protecting Petersburg.

Finally, in January 1865, bad weather cut Petersburg off from Richmond, and those left in Petersburg starved. At the end of March 1865 Lee decided that he had to punch a hole through part of Grant's lines around Petersburg, and then retreat westward with what was left of his army. Richmond's fate—and the outcome of the Civil War—would be determined by this gamble.

Sherman's March to the Sea

Throughout the Confederacy, Union forces were advancing by the summer of 1864. It was not a question of if the South would be defeated but when. Now the war took on a new aspect. General William Tecumseh Sherman led his army through Georgia to take Atlanta. He then marched through to Savannah, destroying everything of value in his path. This campaign, known as the March to the Sea, was brutal but decisive. Sherman would end the Confederacy's ability to fight on by destroying its resources.

While Generals Ulysses S. Grant and Robert E. Lee battered one another's armies like two boxers in the ring in Virginia in the middle of 1864, General William Sherman and Confederate General Joseph Johnston preferred to maneuver. Sherman and Johnston acted like two dancers at a square dance—briefly touching then moving on to another part of the floor. While fighting wore away the Armies of the Potomac and Northern Virginia, Sherman's command, the Armies of the Cumberland, the Ohio, and the Tennessee, and Johnston's Army of Tennessee became experts at marching and digging trenches.

General William Tecumseh Sherman led the Union forces that laid waste to Georgia in 1864.

A War of Maneuver

Sherman began his campaign on May 5, 1864. He moved south from Chattanooga, Tennessee, and found Johnston and his army in front of Dalton, Georgia. Sherman did not think his soldiers could win if they assaulted Johnston's troops. So he let two-thirds of his troops pretend they were going to attack, while the other third marched south through

Snake Creek Gap. This force headed toward Resaca. If these troops captured this town, they would cut the railroad line that brought key supplies to Johnston. The Confederates would be forced to surrender.

There were only 5,000 defenders in Resaca when General James McPherson's 30,000-strong Union Army of the Tennessee arrived on May 9. However, that Confederate force was 5,000 more than McPherson had expected, so he took up a defensive position at Snake Creek Gap to wait for reinforcements. This gave Johnston ample time to move his army out of its strong position and take it south to Resaca. Sherman ordered his army to follow Johnston.

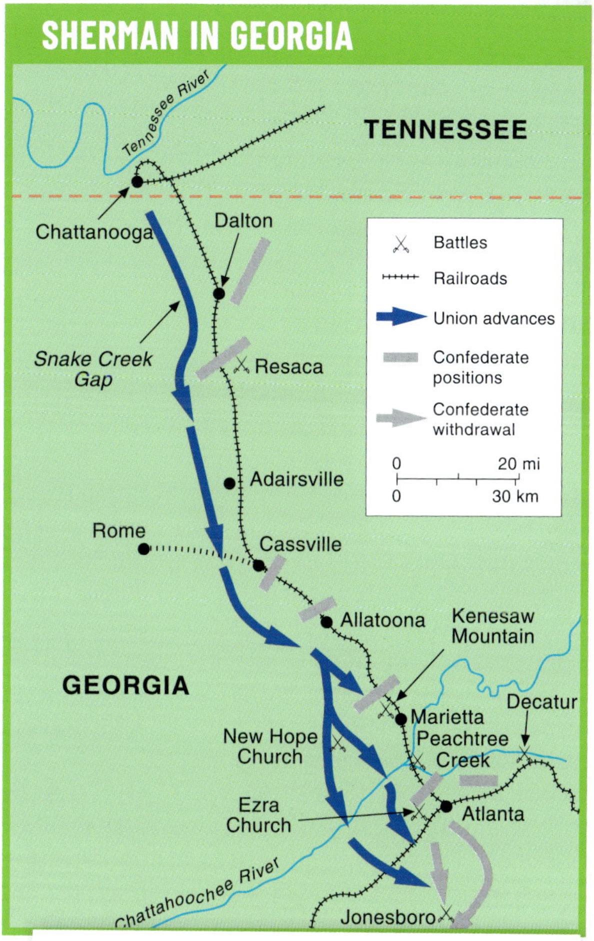

The Union campaign to capture Atlanta in 1864 involved an almost continuous sequence of maneuvers and battles as the Confederates were forced back south from the border between Tennessee and Georgia.

A Slow Retreat

On May 13 Sherman began a three-day assault on Johnston's army at Resaca. The Confederates beat off each attack, but the last one almost turned Johnston's left flank.

The Southern general decided to retreat and fell back toward Adairsville. Sherman repeated the same maneuver here. He sent part of his army around Johnston. While the move through Snake Creek Gap caught Johnston by surprise, this one did not. He was able to retreat once again, but to a better position at Cassville.

Johnston was waiting for an opportunity to catch a part of Sherman's army on the march. He finally had his chance at Cassville. Sherman's army was marching south in three columns. The columns were too far apart to come to one another's aid if attacked. Johnston ordered his army to attack. But one of his corps commanders, General John B. Hood, did not believe the attack would work. He refused to attack, and Johnston had to retreat to the south once again.

Failed Attacks

Johnston now placed his army directly in front of Allatoona. Once again he dared Sherman to attack, but once again Sherman swung his army around Johnston. This time, however, Johnston had sent Hood to take up a defensive position at New Hope Church, where Sherman's forces would have to go if they were to get around behind the main Confederate forces.

The Union soldiers assaulted the Confederates in their trenches three times on May 25, and each of the attacks was driven back with heavy casualties. The attacks were resumed on May 28, but these were defeated as well. Sherman ordered his own army to dig trenches.

For the next four weeks Sherman and Johnston gradually moved their armies southeast. There were no big battles. Sherman might send a division to occupy a hill or a wood, and Johnston would respond by sending a brigade. The outcome of these maneuvers was that the armies ended up in front of Marietta, 20 miles (32 km) northwest of Atlanta. Heavy rains turned the clay roads of this part of the country into slippery tracks that made any march a slow one.

The Confederate Army of Tennessee was now in trenches on Kenesaw Mountain. On June 23, 1864, Sherman ordered an attack. This time 140 Union cannons bombarded the Confederate positions for an hour before General George Thomas's Army of the Cumberland attacked. These Union troops advanced in close order and made an easy target for the Southern defenders. Sherman halted the attacks after 3,000 Union soldiers had been killed or wounded. He then took part of his army and sent it marching around Johnston's force.

On to Atlanta

Sherman was close to Atlanta. Confederate president Jefferson Davis was worried. Atlanta was vital to the Confederacy. It was a center of trade, the hub of a key transportation system, and supplied the Southern armies with weapons. Its capture would be a disaster. Davis had never cared for Johnston, and sent General Braxton Bragg, whom Davis liked, to report on the situation.

Bragg met with Hood, who had failed to attack the Union army at Cassville, as Johnston had wanted. Hood gave Bragg a letter in which Johnston had written: "I regard it as a great misfortune to our country that we failed to give battle to the enemy many miles north of our present position." Bragg reported

WOMEN AT WAR

Women carried out many vital roles for both the North and South during the Civil War. Some worked in war-related industries, such as uniform-making, or took over government jobs vacated by men who had gone to war. Others joined drives to raise war funds or informal circles of friends to send food parcels or warm clothing to the soldiers. Many others, however, took a much more direct involvement, particularly in the fields of nursing care and spying.

In the North Dorothea Dix, a campaigner for prison reform and improved care of the poor and mentally ill before the Civil War, became the superintendent of the Union's corps of nurses and did much to improve the chances of soldiers surviving their battlefield wounds by improving their medical care. Clara Barton became known as the "angel of the battlefield" for the nursing care she showed to soldiers during the Civil War and later was instrumental in founding the National Society of the Red Cross (1881). She also compiled records of dead and missing soldiers until 1869.

Some women in both the North and South also became spies, an occupation that could have led to their execution if caught. One Confederate supporter, Mary Surratt, in whose Washington boardinghouse the plot to assassinate President Lincoln had been hatched, was one of those executed on July 7, 1865, for involvement in the scheme.

Dorothea Dix, who became head of the Union's nursing corps in the war.

this to Davis. On July 17, Davis took Johnston's command away from him and replaced him with General John Hood.

Within two days of taking command, Hood attacked Sherman's army at Peachtree Creek. He wanted to use two corps to attack the Union army commanded by Thomas. However, one of his corps commanders was unhappy with the way his units were deployed. He kept altering their positions all afternoon. Then the commander of the other corps became impatient and started the attack in the late afternoon. The attack at first succeeded, but then the Confederate troops advanced into ravines. Union regiments came up to the edges of the ravines and fired down into the masses of Confederate infantry. The attack came to a halt. The other

THE BATTLE OF MOBILE BAY

Mobile, Alabama, was a major port for Southern ships. It stood at the head of Mobile Bay and was protected by forts. It was also the port where many blockade-runners brought in supplies to the Confederacy.

Admiral David Farragut had wanted to capture it since April 1862, after the surrender of nearby New Orleans (see page 35). It was not until 1864 that he had his chance. His fleet of 12 wooden warships and four ironclad monitors raced past the bombarding guns of Fort Morgan in the late afternoon of August 5. Farragut's fleet also had to pick its way through a minefield. (In those days mines were known as torpedoes.) When his lead ship halted under fire, Farragut demanded to know what was wrong. He was told that torpedoes blocked the way. "Damn the torpedoes, full speed ahead," he shouted.

The torpedoes sunk one monitor, but no other ships. Then the Union fleets had to fight a powerful Confederate ironclad, the *Tennessee*. A lucky shot damaged the *Tennessee's* rudder, and the Southern warship was forced to surrender. Farragut's victory denied the Southern blockade-runners access to Mobile, leaving only the ports of Wilmington and Charleston from which they could sail.

The fierce fighting during the Battle of Mobile Bay, August 5, 1864. Admiral David Farragut pressed home an attack in order to take this strategically important port.

Confederate corps now tried to attack, but Thomas deployed six cannons and directed their fire on this new attack. This, too, came to a halt. Both retreated. Hood had lost nearly 5,000 soldiers for nothing.

Hood decided to try again. This time he sent a whole corps on a long night march to attack the Union Army of the Tennessee at Decatur 5 miles (8 km) east of Atlanta. This corps started late. Then it got caught in a traffic jam as infantry and artillery shared the same road. Then it got lost. An attack that was supposed to start at dawn on July 22

The ruins of an Atlanta railroad after the city was burned to the ground by Sherman's troops. Sherman was determined to destroy the South's ability to wage war.

started at lunchtime. But it hit the wrong part of the Union line. The worst fighting was over a hill, where two brigades battled it out hand-to-hand until nightfall. Hood's last attempt was to strike at the federals at Ezra Church, southwest of Atlanta, on July 28. Some 5,000 Southern soldiers were killed or wounded. Hood had lost many troops, but the federals had been stopped from cutting an important railroad connection.

The Fall of Atlanta

Sherman then began a siege of Atlanta. He had his field artillery bombard it. Finally, the last railroad line bringing food to Hood was cut. Hood decided to retreat from Atlanta after losing a battle at Jonesboro below the city on August 31. Union soldiers marched into Atlanta on September 2.

The fall of Atlanta and the Union naval victory of Mobile Bay, Alabama, on August 5 revived Lincoln's chances for reelection as president. Lincoln faced opposition from within his own Republican Party over the conduct of the war and its aims. Some Southern politicians believed that the Union's recent heavy casualties might cause the election of a candidate who would agree to stop the war. But their hopes were never realized. Lincoln was reelected with 55 percent of the popular vote on November 8, 1864. President Jefferson Davis had never believed in such dreams. He believed that the war would only be won by Confederate victories and was determined to continue fighting.

The March to the Sea

Sherman believed that too. He decided that it was necessary to destroy the Confederate ability and will to fight by destroying the property that the Southern armies claimed they fought for. On November 15, Sherman burned Atlanta to the ground. He then led his army on a march to Savannah.

Sherman's soldiers burned anything they could not use and freed slaves along a Georgia land strip 40 miles (64 km) wide between Savannah and Atlanta. Savannah, a key Southern port, fell on December 21. The war was entering its final months. There was nothing the Confederacy could do to prevent defeat.

Franklin and Nashville

Late in 1864, the Union capture of Atlanta and Sherman's March to the Sea had severely weakened the Confederacy. One of the last throws of the dice was an offensive by General John Hood into Tennessee. Hood hoped to retake Nashville and then unite his army with Lee's Army of Northern Virginia. This was a forlorn hope, however. Southern forces were short of food and ammunition. They also faced Union forces that outnumbered them by tens of thousands. Personal bravery on the battlefield could not save the South.

General John Hood may have abandoned Atlanta to the Union forces on September 1, 1864, but he still had 40,000 soldiers under his command. Hood first used this army to disrupt the railroad line between Chattanooga, Tennessee, and Atlanta. General Sherman relied on this railroad to keep his Union army supplied. He had to lead his troops out of the ruins of Atlanta to chase Hood away from the railroad. Hood then retreated into Alabama.

Sherman's march through Georgia to Savannah was only possible because he had left half of his army in Tennessee to watch Hood. General George Thomas went to Nashville to make his base there. He placed part of his army at Pulaski, Tennessee, to keep an eye on Hood's forces in Alabama. Hood decided on a desperate gamble. First, Nathan Bedford Forrest's Confederate cavalry raided into Tennessee to disrupt Northern supply lines and scatter Union forces. On October 11, for example, Forrest attacked Fort Donelson but was beaten off.

Marching to Tennessee

After Forrest returned from his hit-and-run campaign, Hood began marching north into Tennessee in the middle of November. His army consisted of 39,000 battle-hardened soldiers, some of the best that were still fighting for the Confederacy. Hood dreamed of winning a great victory in Tennessee, then going east across the Appalachian Mountains to link up with General Robert E. Lee's Army of Northern Virginia. Together, Hood and Lee might have defeated Grant and Sherman. In truth, the plan was far too ambitious and had little real chance of success.

Hood's Desperate Gamble

Hood crossed over the Tennessee River in Alabama and marched north into Tennessee. He first tried to defeat the Union force commanded by General John Schofield on November 14.

Schofield was under orders from Thomas to use his Union troops to delay Hood's march on Nashville. Hood marched around Schofield's flank and placed his army at Columbia. However, Schofield was able to escape Hood's trap on November 26–27, and Schofield's army then withdrew toward Franklin, 15 miles (24 km) to the south of Nashville.

Hood followed Schofield quickly. He was very angry with his troops. Hood believed they had forgotten how to attack because General Joseph Johnston, their previous commander, had always placed them in strong defensive positions, forcing the Union troops to attack them. So, at Franklin, Hood ordered them to charge Schofield's lines. The Southern soldiers knew that they would be fired at by thousands of Union troops as they crossed the open fields to attack the Northern lines. But November 30, 1864, they did it anyway.

Almost 7,000 of the 27,000 Confederate troops who attacked at Franklin were killed or wounded. Many important Southern officers were also killed, more than in any other battle of the entire war. The South could not afford to have its few remaining veteran officers and soldiers thrown away in ill-judged attacks that had little chance of success. In contrast, Schofield had 2,300 men killed or wounded out of his force of 32,000.

Schofield led his troops from Franklin to Nashville, where they linked up with Thomas and his army. The Union forces there now numbered 60,000. Hood had little more than 20,000 soldiers left as he headed for Nashville, which he

General John Hood's Confederate troops charge into a storm of Union rifle and artillery fire during the Battle of Franklin on November 30, 1864.

finally reached on December 2.

Hood Defeated

The defenses surrounding Nashville were some of the strongest in the country, even better than the ones the Confederates had constructed around Petersburg. Hood finally recognized that an attack on the heavily defended city would be a waste of time. However, Thomas, the "Rock of Chickamauga," was preparing to launch an attack of his own on Hood. Bad weather and the need to train a large number of new recruits kept Thomas from attacking the Confederate forces outside Nashville for two weeks.

When Thomas did attack, on December 15, his troops were at first held back by the outnumbered Southern troops. On the next day, however, the Union troops attacked again. The left flank and center of the Southern line gave way, leaving just the right flank to protect the retreating Southerners. Thomas's army, some 50,000 men, suffered about 3,000 casualties, while Hood had over 5,000 men out of 31,000 killed, wounded, or taken prisoner. Hood was finally relieved of his command in January 1865. His army, one of the last available to the South, had been destroyed.

After the destruction of Hood's army at the Battle of Nashville, the only serious resistance to final Union victory would come from Robert E. Lee and what remained of the Army of Northern Virginia. Lee's command, although short of supplies, was willing to fight but it faced enormous odds. Union armies were closing in from all directions in great strength.

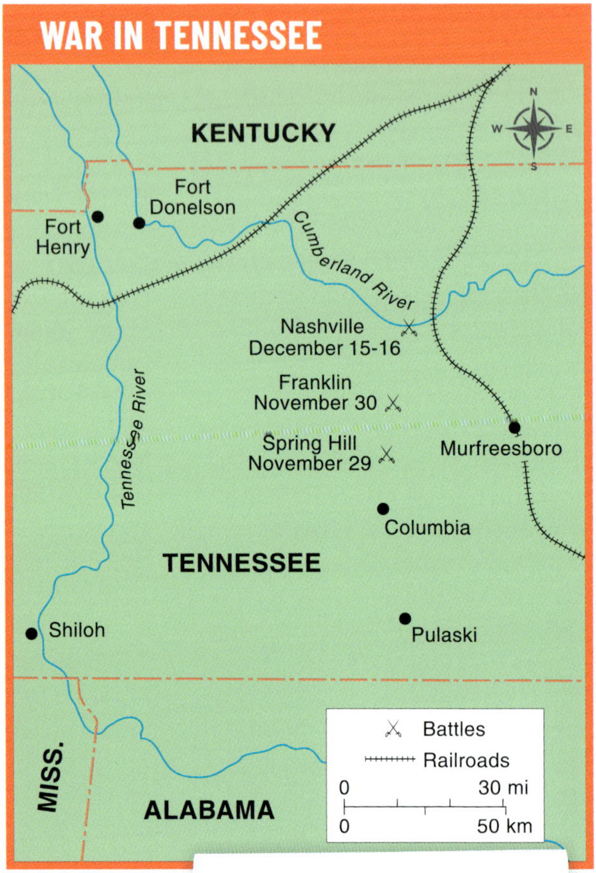

The Battles of Franklin and Nashville in late 1864 resulted in the destruction of one of the South's last remaining armies.

AFRICAN AMERICANS AT WAR

Although the South did not seriously consider using its enslaved population as soldiers until the final months of the war, they did contribute to the war effort. Without them the plantations and farms would not have been able to feed the Confederate armies, and the South's industries would not have received the weapons and equipment they needed. African Americans also worked with armies in the field as teamsters, drovers, blacksmiths, and the like. They also built the fortifications that protected many of the South's major ports.

The North made great use of freed or escaped enslaved people. About 200,000 "contrabands" worked as teamsters, cooks, and laborers with Northern armies. African Americans in the North also took part in the fighting itself. The Militia Act of July 1862 allowed President Lincoln to recruit soldiers from "persons of African descent" into the Union's armies.

The first African American soldiers to fight belonged to a Kansas regiment. They fought in a skirmish in Missouri in October 1862. The first striking wartime examples of African American valor were given by two regiments raised by the abolitionist governor of Massachusetts, John Andrew.

One of them, the 54th Massachusetts, gained lasting fame for its attack on Fort Wagner, South Carolina, in July 1863. Many of the regiment were killed in a brave but finally unsuccessful attack. One of the survivors became the first African American to be awarded the Congressional Medal of Honor. The bravery of the 54th Massachusetts did much to convince those in the North that African American soldiers were fit for much more active combat and should not be used solely for garrison duties as some commanders believed.

African American units fought with great bravery in such key moments as the Vicksburg campaign and the Battle of Nashville. In total, 186,000 African Americans fought in federal armies during the war, while probably another 20,000 served with the U.S. Navy. Only 87 were commissioned as officers, however.

Colonel Robert Shaw, with sword in hand, falls mortally wounded as he leads the gallant attack by the 54th Massachusetts on Fort Wagner, July 1863.

Saving the Union

Throughout the spring of 1865, tired and hungry Confederate troops had vainly tried to defeat the Union armies as they marched on Richmond or sought out the few remaining centers of resistance. Then, on April 9, 1865, Robert E. Lee surrendered his Army of Northern Virginia to General Grant. The final Confederate fighting force surrendered on May 26. By then, however, President Abraham Lincoln had been assassinated by John Wilkes Booth, a Confederate sympathizer.

At the end of March 1865 General Robert E. Lee realized he could no longer remain in Petersburg, as the long Union siege was getting close to success. Although withdrawing from Petersburg would mean that Richmond was almost certain to fall, it was a sacrifice that Lee had to make to keep the Army of Northern Virginia a viable military force in the field.

There were three reasons why Lee took this decision. First, bad weather had severed the links between Petersburg and Richmond, so he could get no supplies from there. Second, on January 15 a Union force had captured Fort Fisher, which protected Wilmington, North Carolina. Much of Lee's supplies came through this seaport. Third, during February General Sherman had led his troops north through South Carolina. His soldiers destroyed everything just as they had in Georgia. Lee decided that Sherman had to be stopped and that it would take what little was left of the Army of Northern Virginia to do it.

Sherman in the Carolinas

President Jefferson Davis made Lee the general-in-chief of all the remaining Confederate armies in February. On February 22, Lee gave General Joseph Johnston command of the forces trying to stop Sherman. However, Sherman and his troops had finally occupied Columbia, South Carolina's capital, on February 17, 1865. That night the town was destroyed by fire.

Sherman pressed on into North Carolina, aiming at the town of Goldsboro (see map, page 9). Just as Johnston had tried, while defending Atlanta, to catch part of Sherman's army with all of his own, so he tried here. Once again he succeeded. On March 19, at Bentonville, North Carolina (see map, page 9), his attack succeeded in halting the Union advance. But it could not break the Union line. Sherman rushed toward the battlefield and

The bombardment of Fort Fisher, North Carolina. The key fort was captured on January 15, 1865, by a force of sailors, marines, and army troops. Fort Fisher protected the harbor at Wilmington, one of the last ports through which armaments from Europe could reach Lee's army.

reached it on March 21. Johnston retreated. Bentonville was the last important Confederate effort to stop Sherman's advance.

Lee's Last Gamble

Lee's attempt to break out of Petersburg began with an attack on Fort Stedman, part of the Union network of trenches outside the city. If the line could be broken through here, then the Confederate garrison would be able to raid supply depots just behind it. The soldiers would carry off what they could and destroy the rest. The attack was also being made away from the direction in which Lee wanted to move the rest of his army. Grant might weaken the western end of his line to reinforce the eastern area around Fort Stedman and make it easier for Lee to carry out his strategic retreat.

The attack was made just before dawn on March 25. The fort fell quickly. The Confederates used a trick to gain entrance. A few soldiers went forward claiming they were deserting. When the unsuspecting Union soldiers let them into the fort, the Southern troops took control.

Despite the initial success at Fort Stedman, the Confederates were thrown out of the fort by veteran Union troops after a bitter fight lasting four hours. At the end of the battle Lee had suffered 3,500 casualties, Grant only 1,000. Lee could not afford to lose so many of his best troops, and his plan to draw off Grant's troops had also failed. Grant, with over 120,000 men facing less than 60,000 Confederates, was ready to finish off Lee's army.

Grant sent a strong force of two cavalry divisions and an infantry corps, commanded by General Philip Sheridan, to march to the southwest of Petersburg. This would block Lee's route to the Carolinas. Lee in turn sent General George Pickett with two divisions to stop Sheridan. Pickett was able to check Sheridan's advance on March 30–31. The two armies met again, at Five Forks, just southwest of Petersburg, on April 1. Pickett had gone to a party, believing Sheridan would not attack. Sheridan did just that. After a hard fight the Southern troops were defeated. Half of them were captured.

Robert E. Lee surrenders his Army of Northern Virginia to Ulysses S. Grant at Appomattox Court House on April 9, 1865.

Assault on Petersburg

Grant took another chance that Lee's army was beaten. On April 2, he ordered a general assault on Petersburg. All along the line the Union infantrymen got up out of their trenches and charged toward the Southern defenses. Lee's soldiers fought hard, but only to gain time. They held off the Federal attacks. Then, on April 3, Lee and his soldiers abandoned Petersburg. That same day, Union troops entered Richmond, which formally surrendered. President Lincoln visited the city on the next day.

Lee's army headed west and met with the garrison from Richmond at the village of Amelia Springs. On April 5, they began a race against a force commanded by Sheridan. Lee tried to keep his soldiers moving quickly in order to turn south. Sheridan just kept ahead of Lee so that when Lee's force turned south, Union troops could block its path.

Lee kept trying though. His soldiers had not been eating properly for months and could not outrun Sheridan's better-fed troops. On April 9, Lee found two Union infantry corps in front of him and two coming up quickly behind. He was trapped on April 9, and feeling that further resistance was useless, chose to surrender. Grant met him in the parlor of a house at Appomattox Court House, where the two generals worked out surrender terms. Further south, Johnston surrendered to Sherman on April 26. On May 26, the last Confederate general, Edmund Kirby Smith, finally surrendered.

Jefferson Davis was captured near Irwinville, Georgia, on May 10. He was put in prison, where he remained until 1867. Then he was released and allowed to live out the rest of his life without standing

LINCOLN'S ASSASSINATION

President Abraham Lincoln decided to go to Ford's Theater in Washington on April 14, 1865. His plans were known to a small group of Confederates who had been attempting to kidnap or kill him during the war. One of them, John Wilkes Booth, was an actor. Since he was known to the people who worked in the theater, he easily gained access to the building. He then went to the box where the president was sitting and shot him in the head. Booth jumped down to the stage, damaging one of his legs. He reportedly shouted, "Sic semper tyrannis!" (Latin for "Thus be it ever to all tyrants!") and ran off into the night.

Meanwhile, a man entered the house of Secretary of State William Seward and attempted to stab him to death. Seward's life was saved by an iron brace he wore to protect his jaw, broken in a recent accident. Another man was supposed to kill Vice President Andrew Johnson, but got drunk. Booth was eventually tracked down in Port Royal, Virginia. Refusing to surrender, he was shot.

Southern sympathizer John Wilkes Booth (left) about to assassinate Lincoln.

trial for treason. The victorious president, Abraham Lincoln, knew nothing of all this. On April 14, 1865, while watching a play in Washington, D.C., Lincoln was shot by an angry pro-Confederate actor named John Wilkes Booth. Lincoln died the following morning. However, the war was over and the Union had been preserved.

Glossary

bullet A missile fired from a musket. Unlike the round musket ball, a bullet is slightly longer and shaped at one end like a cone. The more streamlined shape allows the bullet to travel farther with much greater accuracy.

communications Transmitted information; in wartime military information between units and their headquarters; during the Civil War by courier, balloon-observation, flags, and telegraphy.

conscription Compulsory enrollment of able-bodied persons in a country's armed forces, usually during a national emergency.

ironclad A 19th century armored warship. A typical ironclad was built of wood and powered by a steam engine. The wooden part of the ship above water was covered in a shell of iron, which protected it from gunfire. Most early ironclads were underpowered and unseaworthy, but could outfight a warship built of wood only.

mine An explosive device (usually concealed), designed to destroy an enemy's vehicles, ships, or personnel.

monitor A type of warship fitted with one or more revolving turrets with one or more guns.

rifling A technique used on both rifle and artillery barrels that allowed weapons to fire farther and with greater accuracy. Rifled barrels were made with spiral grooves cut into the inside of the barrels. These gave a bullet or shell spin when fired, leading to a greater range and accuracy.

torpedo A weapon for destroying ships. Unlike modern self-propelled torpedoes, those used in the Civil War consisted of an explosive device fitted to a long wooden spar. The spar was attached to a small vessel, which was directed at and sailed toward a target. The spar-mounted explosive device detonated on contact with the target.

volunteer A civilian who agrees to fight in time of war, often for a cause, adventure, or an enlistment fee (a sum of money paid on volunteering to fight). While enthusiastic, volunteers usually lack military skills and combat experience.

war of attrition A military strategy based on the idea of grinding down an enemy's armies and war industries until they are no longer able to continue to fight. For both sides, it usually involves heavy casualties and large-scale destruction.

Further Reading

Abnett, Dan. *Civil War Battles: Graphic Short Stories*. Rosen Publishing, 2024.

Boutland, Craig. *The Civil War: Timelines, Facts, and Battles*. Rosen Publishing, 2023.

Idsikowski, Lisa. *The Real Story Behind the Civil War*. Rosen Publishing, 2020.

Kerry, Isaac. *The Attack of Fort Sumter: A Day That Changed America*. Capstone, 2023.

Lerner Publications. *Hidden Heroes in the Civil War*. Lerner, 2023.

Websites

civilwar.si.edu
The Smithsonian Institution's Civil War collections, with essays, images, and other primary sources.

kidsnationalgeographic.com/history/article/gettysburg
Introduction to this key battle.

pbs.org/civilwar
PBS site supporting the Ken Burns production *The Civil War*.

Index